AIR  **RT 2/94**

Air Accidents Investigation Branch

Department of Transport

Report on the accident involving
Royal Air Force Tornado GR1, ZG 754
and Bell 206B JetRanger III, G-BHYW
at Farleton Knott near Kendal, Cumbria
on 23 June 1993

This investigation was carried out in accordance with
*The Air Navigation (Investigation of Air Accidents involving Civil
and Military Aircraft or Installations) Regulations 1986*

London: HMSO

ISBN 0 11 551283 7

LIST OF RECENT AIRCRAFT ACCIDENT REPORTS ISSUED BY AIR ACCIDENTS INVESTIGATION BRANCH

3/92	De Havilland DHC-7, G-BOAW, between Brussels and London City Airport, on 30 January 1991	July 1992
4/92	British Aerospace ATP, G-BMYK, 10 miles north of COWLY, near Oxford, on 11 August 1991	October 1992
5/92	British Aerospace ATP, G-LOGA, at Edinburgh Airport, Scotland, on 5 February 1992	October 1992
6/92	British Aerospace ATP, G-BTPE, at Sumburgh Airport, Shetland Islands, on 23 December 1991	December 1992
1/93	Piper PA-28-161 Cadet, G-BPJT, at Oxford Airport, Kidlington, on 12 July 1992	April 1993
2/93	AS 332L Super Puma, G-TIGH, near the Cormorant 'A' platform, East Shetland Basin, on 14 March 1992	May 1993
3/93	Lockheed 1011 Tristar, 9Y-TGJ, near 'KIRN' VOR, Germany, on 9 March 1992	June 1993
4/93	British Aerospace 146-300, G-UKHP, at Aberdeen Airport, Dyce, Scotland, on 31 March 1992	August 1993
5/93	British Aircraft Corporation/SNIAS Concorde 102, G-BOAB, over the North Atlantic, on 21 March 1992	November 1993
1/94	Aerospatiale AS355F1 Twin Squirrel, G-OHMS Near Llanbedr Airfield, Gwynedd, on 8 December 1992	January 1994

These Reports are available from HMSO Bookshops and Accredited Agents

Department of Transport
Air Accidents Investigation Branch
Defence Research Agency
Farnborough
Hampshire GU14 6TD

5 May 1994

The Right Honourable John MacGregor
Secretary of State for Transport

Sir,

I have the honour to submit the report by Mr R StJ Whidborne, an Inspector of Air Accidents, on the circumstances of the mid-air collision between RAF Tornado GR1, ZG 754 and Agusta Bell 206B JetRanger III, G-BHYW that occurred at Farleton Knott near Kendal, Cumbria, on 23 June 1993.

I have the honour to be
Sir
Your obedient servant

K P R Smart
Chief Inspector of Air Accidents

Department of Transport
Air Accidents Investigation Branch
Defence Research Agency
Farnborough
Hampshire GU14 6TD

5 May 1994

The Right Honourable Malcolm Riftkind
Secretary of State for Defence

Sir,

I have the honour to submit the report by Mr R StJ Whidborne, an Inspector of Air Accidents, on the circumstances of the mid-air collision between RAF Tornado GR1, ZG 754 and Agusta Bell 206B JetRanger III, G-BHYW that occurred at Farleton Knott near Kendal, Cumbria, on 23 June 1993.

I have the honour to be
Sir
Your obedient servant

K P R Smart
Chief Inspector of Air Accidents

Contents

Page

GLOSSARY OF ABBREVIATIONS USED IN THIS REPORT

AAIB	-	Air Accidents Investigation Branch
AAR	-	Aircraft Accident Report
ADR	-	Accident data Recorder
AIC	-	Aeronautical Information Circular
AIP	-	Aeronautical Information Publication
AIS	-	Aeronautical Information Service
ALFENS	-	Automatic Low Flying Enquiry and Notification System
ANO	-	Air Navigation Order
AOC	-	Air Operator's Certificate
ASI	-	Airspeed Indicator
ATC	-	Air Traffic Control
AWR	-	Air to ground Weapons Range
ATIS	-	Automatic terminal Information Service
BASI	-	Bureau of Air Safety Investigation
CAA	-	Civil Aviation Authority
CANP	-	Civil Aircraft Notification Procedure
CAP	-	Civil Aviation Publication
CCF	-	Coordinated Control Function
CVR	-	Cockpit Voice Recorder
CWS	-	Collision Warning System
DRA	-	Defence Research Agency
DUA	-	Dedicated User Area
FDR	-	Flight Data Recorder
FJ	-	Fast Jet (major portion of flight >300 kts IAS)
GA	-	General Aviation
HISL	-	High Intensity Strobe Lights
IAM	-	Institute of Aviation Medicine
ICAO	-	International Civil Aviation Organisation
JAS	-	Joint Airmiss Section
JAWG	-	Joint Airmiss Working Group
JSP	-	Joint Service Publication
LATCC	-	London Air Traffic Control Centre
MATZ	-	Military Air Traffic Zone
MATS	-	Manual of Air Traffic Services
mb	-	millibars
MHz	-	Mega Hertz
MOD	-	Ministry of Defence
MSD	-	Minimum Separation Distance
NATS	-	National Air Traffic Services
nm	-	nautical miles
NOTAM	-	Notice to Airmen

OM	-	Operations Manual
PAPI	-	Precision Approach Path Indicator
PINS	-	Pipeline Inspection Notification Procedure
QNH	-	Corrected mean sea level pressure
SRA	-	Surveillance Approach Radar
TBC	-	Tactical Booking Cell
TCAS	-	Traffic Alerting and Collision Avoidance System
TDP	-	Technology Demonstrator Programme
UHF	-	Ultra High Frequency
UKLFB	-	UK Low Flying Handbook
UTC	-	Co-ordinated Universal Time
VHF	-	Very High Frequency
VMC	-	Visual Meteorological Conditions

Air Accidents Investigation Branch

Aircraft Accident Report No: 2/94   (EW/E93/6/1)

Aircraft: 1

Registered Owner and Operator:	Lakeside Helicopters Limited
Aircraft Type:	Agusta Bell 206B JetRanger III
Nationality:	British
Registration:	G-BHYW

Aircraft: 2

Operator:	Royal Air Force (RAF)
Type:	British Aerospace (BAe) Tornado
Model:	GR1
Registration:	ZG 754
Place of Accident:	Farleton Knott, near Kendal, Cumbria
Date and Time:	23 June 1993 at 1049 hrs

All times in this report are UTC

Synopsis

The accident was notified to the Air Accidents Investigation Branch (AAIB) at 1225 hrs on 23 June 1993 and an investigation began the same day. The AAIB team comprised Mr R StJ Whidborne (Investigator in Charge), Mr D S Miller (Operations), Mr S W Moss (Engineering) and Miss A Evans (Engineering). An RAF Board of Inquiry was also convened under Service Regulations.

The Bell 206B JetRanger III helicopter, which was based at Edinburgh, Scotland, was engaged on an aerial pipeline inspection flight. The Tornado GR1, based at RAF Bruggen,

1

Germany, was one of a pair of Tornados on a routine low level training flight in transit from the east coast weapons ranges, via the Lake District, to RAF Leuchars in Scotland.

The collision occurred over open ground at a height of 380 feet agl, some 500 metres to the north west of the higher ground of Farleton Fell, close to Dove House farm near Kendal. After the collision the helicopter, with its tail rotor and boom severed aft of the horizontal stabiliser, entered a series of spiral turns before descending out of control. The helicopter pilot and passenger were killed on impact with the ground. The Tornado, although substantially damaged, diverted to the BAe airfield at Warton and landed without further incident.

Immediately before the accident the JetRanger had carried out one left-hand orbit at an estimated height of 300 feet above ground level (agl) and at a speed of 40 kt overhead some engineering sub-contractors working close to the pipeline. Eyewitness evidence indicates that the JetRanger had just rolled 'wings level' onto a northerly heading when, at 1049 hrs, it was struck by the Tornado which was flying low level on a north westerly heading at a speed of 450 kt.

The report identifies the following causal factors:

      (i)   Neither pilot saw the other aircraft in time to avoid the collision.

      (ii)   Incompatibility of operational modes and the unsuitability of the 'see-and-avoid' principle in these circumstances failed to ensure the necessary separation.

      (iii)   There were no routine procedures, such as CANP, or facilities, such as CWS, to inform either pilot about the presence of the other aircraft prior to the impact.

Five safety recommendations were made on 28 September 1993 and a further five are made in Part 4 of this report.

1   Factual Information

1.1   History of the flights

1.1.1   JetRanger

The Agusta Bell 206B JetRanger III was owned and operated by an Edinburgh based helicopter company with contracts for three major UK chemical suppliers to conduct, on a regular basis, routine aerial inspections of their UK pipeline networks. Inspections of the UK Ethylene pipeline from Stanlow to Grangemouth were carried out in accordance with the powers conferred on the Health and Safety Executive (HSE)[1]. The inspections, which were carried out fortnightly, over a three day period, were conducted at heights mainly between 300 feet and 700 feet agl and at a speed of approximately 60 kt. Pipeline superintendents, representing the responsible chemical company, accompanied the pilot on each flight to act as an observer.

At 0730 hrs the helicopter pilot left Standish and transited to Barton Airfield landing at 0736 hrs to collect the pipeline superintendent for that day. Prior to departure from Barton the pilot made a brief visit to Lancashire Aero Club, where meteorological and navigational information was displayed, to pay his landing fee and 'book out' for the first stage of the flight to Blackpool. There was no requirement for him to notify the relevant authorities of his exact route, timings or operating heights as the flight would be operating outside controlled airspace and in accordance with the operator's low flying exemption.

At 0805 hrs the pilot and observer, occupying the right and left-hand seats respectively left Barton Airfield and flew the usual route via Runcorn, St Helens, and Skelmersdale. They passed to the west of Preston maintaining routine radio contact with the Air Traffic Control (ATC) units at Liverpool and Warton. Where the route crossed the M55 motorway they departed from the pipeline and flew directly to Blackpool Airport arriving at 0936 hrs. The helicopter was then refuelled and the pilot and observer had some light refreshments.

At 1019 hrs the helicopter took off on the next phase of its inspection, following the pipeline which runs parallel to the M6 motorway, displaced approximately 5 kms to the west, and crossing the motorway at Junction 33. The pipeline then routes northbound parallel with the motorway displaced approximately 1 km to the east. Just to the south of Junction 36 the pipeline routes close to the motorway and alongside the Lancaster canal, approximately 500 metres west of the higher ground of Farleton Fell.

---

1   In accordance with sections 20 and 23 of the Pipe-lines Act 1962 as amended by the Pipe-lines Act (Repeals and Modifications) Regulations 1974.

Three engineering sub-contractors, working in this area, knew that the pipeline was to be surveyed by helicopter and, at approximately 1050 hrs, they saw the helicopter as it approached from the south. They reported that the weather at the time was 'clear, sunny and fine with good visibility, enough to see the Lake District hills'. The helicopter appeared to be flying at its normal survey height and, as it approached the working party, it circled their position in a left-hand orbit so that the observer could have good sight of the ground and the work being carried out.

The ground workers stopped working, waved, and were able to see clearly the face of the observer who was waving back. Having completed the orbit the helicopter rolled out in a level attitude at about 300 to 400 feet and proceeded northbound. Moments later it was hit by the Tornado.

1.1.2   Tornado

The Tornado GR1 was engaged on a routine low level training flight intending to land at RAF Leuchars, Scotland. At 0944 hrs on Wednesday 23 June 1993 it departed RAF Bruggen to fly as No 2 of a pair of Tornados on a sortie involving various bombing profile manoeuvres using either the Donna Nook Air-to-ground Weapons Range (AWR) or Cowden AWR on the east coast of the UK. With the range work complete the crews planned to carry out a low level attack transit flight landing at RAF Leuchars to refuel, before returning to RAF Bruggen later that day.

The outbound and return flights to RAF Leuchars had been planned the previous day by the formation lead crew and a crew nominated to fly as No 2 of the pair but which, for administrative reasons, comprised a different captain on the day of the accident (see paragraph 1.5.2.3). The Notices to Airmen (NOTAMs), Civil Aircraft Notification Procedures (CANP) and navigational warnings for the route were checked during this initial planning stage and again the following morning prior to their briefing.

The aircraft had planned to take off as a pair but a minor technical problem delayed the No 2's departure. Approximately 15 minutes after his leader, the No 2 aircraft, now fully serviceable and with its anti-collision lights selected on, departed and transited at high level towards the UK east coast bombing ranges. As the Donna Nook AWR was not available, due to other traffic, the No 2 aircraft proceeded direct to Cowden range and joined up with his leader.

With their range work complete the pair set out on the low level portion of the flight to RAF Leuchars with the No 2 flying on the leader's left. During the initial transit the two aircraft maintained a lateral separation of about 4,000 metres. The formation then turned left towards Kendal and in doing so the No 2 changed sides and flew on the leader's right. At this stage of the flight the pilot reported that visibility at low level was excellent.

The first significant turn along the route was to be to the right, around the town of Kendal. The navigator of the No 2 aircraft, reminded his pilot of this track change three minutes before the turn. At this point the Tornado crews were following a route parallel with the A65 trunk road displaced approximately 3 nm to the south. As they approached the high ground of Farleton Knott the pilot of the No 2 aircraft decided to fly tactically by following the A65 valley passing to the north of the high ground of Farleton Knott. This put him on a slightly converging course with his leader who was displaced approximately 4,000 metres to the south and who flew to the south of Farleton Knott. As he entered the valley the pilot of the No 2 aircraft, now surrounded by high ground, lost sight of his leader and concentrated on ensuring that the track ahead was clear. He had to climb initially to avoid a flock of birds but soon resumed his normal height above ground level (below 600 feet with 250 feet MSD). As he reached the end of the valley he satisfied himself that the area ahead was clear. Still on a converging course with his leader and knowing that they were soon to initiate a turn, he looked to the left for the other aircraft. The navigator, in the rear seat and whose forward vision is normally restricted by aircraft equipment, was concentrating his lookout to the right towards the Kendal area where the chart showed an active hang glider site. The pilot reported that, as he glanced to his left, there was a loud bang. Presuming that his aircraft had suffered a bird strike and, noticing significant damage to the radome, the pilot immediately assured the navigator that he still had control of the aircraft and initiated a climb.

Numerous eyewitnesses saw the accident but few saw the Tornado before it hit the JetRanger. None of them noticed any sudden change in attitude or flight path of the helicopter or Tornado to suggest any attempt to avoid a collision. Neither crew of either Tornado saw the helicopter before or after the accident. The navigator of the No 2 aircraft did, however, see something impact the pilot's right quarter light and a blur disappearing down the right wing.

1.1.3   The collision

The collision occurred at a height just below 400 feet agl with the Tornado flying at a ground speed of 440 kt on a heading of 304° and the helicopter flying at a speed estimated to be 60 kt on a heading of 036°. Following the impact, which severed the tail boom of the helicopter just aft of the horizontal stabiliser, several witnesses saw light debris fall from the helicopter as it entered a series of three descending spirals to the right before stabilising at about 150 feet. It then fell vertically to the ground in an upright attitude.

After the impact the No 2 Tornado, assisted by the pair leader, diverted to the BAe airfield at Warton. The aircraft had suffered damage to the right engine, right-hand engine intake and considerable damage to the nose section. The right-hand engine had caught fire but had extinguished itself. During their single engine diversion to Warton the crew of the No 2 aircraft had to rely on the leader for speed and height information as their flight instrumentation had been damaged in the impact.

The Tornado landed without further incident. When the crew examined their aircraft they discovered metal fragments embedded in the nose section. It was only at this time that they realised they had been involved in a mid-air collision with another aircraft.

1.2 Injuries to persons

		Crew	Passengers	Others
1.2.1	JetRanger			
	Fatal	1	1	-
	Serious	-	-	-
	Minor/None	-	-	
1.2.2	Tornado			
	Fatal	-	-	-
	Serious	-	-	-
	Minor/None	2	-	

1.3 Damage to aircraft

JetRanger: Destroyed

Tornado: Substantially damaged (Category 3)

6

1.4   Other damage

Minor damage to farm boundary hedgerow.

1.5   Personnel information

1.5.1	Bell 206B Pilot:	Male, aged 37 years
	Licence:	Airline Transport Pilot's Licence (Helicopters and Gyroplanes), Instructors Rating
	Medical Certificate:	A Class 1 Medical Certificate, with a condition that the holder must wear correcting spectacles, issued on 10 March 1993 and valid until 30 September 1993
	Certificate of Test:	Re-issued on 31 March 1993 and valid until 30 April 1994
	Total flying hours:	4,868
	Total hours on type:	343

1.5.1.1   Operational experience

The pilot was hired by the helicopter company on a freelance basis and had been flight checked in March 1993 by the company Chief Pilot, and Line checked in May 1993 by a company training captain. The pilot had flown pipeline inspection flights for the company on seven previous occasions and was assessed as being competent to act as pilot by day for public transport operations on all operational tasks including powerline and pipeline patrols.

1.5.1.2   Flight duties

On Monday 21 June 1993, after a working weekend, the pilot departed Edinburgh on the three day inspection programme flying for 2 hours and 35 minutes on the pipeline route between Grangemouth and Teesside. The following day he flew south-westwards for 3 hours from Teesside via Liverpool to Standish near Wigan where he spent a quiet night with friends. On 23 June 1993 the pilot was tasked with inspection of the UK Ethylene pipeline from Stanlow, near Liverpool, to Grangemouth. Combined refuelling and rest stops were planned, at Blackpool and Carlisle, as the helicopter headed northwards along this route.

7

1.5.2	Tornado crew	
1.5.2.1	Captain:	Male, aged 25 years. RAF pilot
	Medical examination:	23 April 1992
	Instrument flight check:	22 March 1993, valid until March 1994
	Competency check:	19 April 1993
	Total pilot hours:	718
	Total hours on type:	421
	Total hours last 30 days:	22
1.5.2.2	Navigator:	Male, aged 28 years. RAF Navigator
	Medical examination:	30 March 1993
	Instrument flight check:	Not applicable
	Competency check:	24 November 1992, valid until November 1993
	Total flying hours:	1,047
	Total hours on type	831
	Total hours last 6 months:	72

1.5.2.3 Flight duties

On the day of the accident the original pilot of the No 2 aircraft was delayed on other duties and was replaced, late in the morning. Although the crew composition was changed the replacement (accident) pilot, who had flown a similar sortie profile earlier in the week, was well briefed and had sufficient time to acquaint himself with the sortie contents. Before walking to the aircraft a squadron flight commander informed the pilot that there were no late navigational warnings and confirmed with him that he had had sufficient time to prepare for the flight and was confident to undertake the task.

1. 6   Aircraft Information

1.6.1   Agusta Bell 206B JetRanger III

The helicopter was a single turbine-engined machine of conventional arrangement comprising a two-bladed main rotor and two-bladed tail rotor. It could carry a maximum of five persons and was normally flown from the right-hand seat.

Type:	Agusta Bell 206B JetRanger III
Engine:	1 Allison 250 C20 turboshaft
Constructors Number:	8043
Date of Manufacture:	1968
Certificate of Registration:	Lakeside Helicopters Ltd [2]
Certificate of Airworthiness:	Transport Category (Passenger). Expiry date 8 June 1996
Certificate of Maintenance Review:	8 June 1994 at 11,059.55 hours
Total Airframe hours (at accident):	approximately 11,110
Maximum total weight authorised:	3,200 lb
Estimated weight at time of accident:	2,480 lb
Centre of Gravity at time of accident:	within approved limits

The helicopter's predominant colour was white with dark metallic grey stripes sweeping rearwards to the tailboom. A red/white High Intensity Strobe Light (HISL) was fitted above the cabin on top of the engine oil reservoir and heat exchanger fairing to the rear of the main rotor assembly. Normal white strobe lights were fitted at the tip of each horizontal stabiliser.

The aircraft's technical documentation showed that it had been maintained to the approved Light Aircraft Maintenance Schedule as required by the Certificate of Airworthiness. There were no relevant Carried Forward Defects listed in the Technical Log.

---

[2]   The company ceased trading shortly after the accident.

1.6.2   Tornado

The Panavia Tornado aircraft involved in the accident was a GR1 model bearing the serial number ZG 754 and carried a crew of two. It was fitted with an external 1,500 litre fuel tank on each of its inboard wing pylons and another on its right-hand fuselage pylon. Stores were attached to each of the outboard wing pylons and the left fuselage pylon. Painted in overall grey/green camouflage, it displayed anti-collision lights[3] above and below the fuselage. The radar system fitted to this aircraft was not intended to be used for acquiring or warning of the presence of other aircraft.

1.7   Meteorological information

1.7.1   Forecast

The lead crew and the navigator of the No 2 Tornado attended a weather briefing at 0730 hrs on the morning of the accident. The crews repeated the weather briefing late in the morning, during the main sortie briefing, for the benefit of the replacement No 2 pilot.

The helicopter pilot had the opportunity to study valid weather information, which was displayed at Barton Airfield, when he booked out his flight.

The low level forecast for Scotland and northern England on 23 June 1993 for the period 0600 hrs to 1200 hrs with little change forecast until 1800 hrs was:

Visibility:	30 km, reducing to 7 km in isolated areas in the east
Cloud:	Broken cumulus and stratocumulus, base 2,500 feet and scattered altocumulus base 12,000 feet
Surface wind:	North westerly light
Temperature:	+13°C

1.7.2   Aftercast

An aftercast was prepared by the Meteorological Office, Bracknell for the area of the accident site at 1055 hrs on 23 June 1993. The synoptic situation showed a light and unstable north westerly airstream established over the Lake District with a mean sea level pressure of 1,017 mb.

Visibility:	30 km or more

---

3   Approximate light output of 400 candela.

Weather:	Nil
Cloud:	Scattered cumulus base between 2,000 and 2,500 feet with scattered, occasionally broken, strato-cumulus base around 4,000 feet.
Surface wind:	300°/07 kt
Temperature:	+14°C
Sun's position:	azimuth 146° (True), elevation 55° 17'

1.7.3   Witness observations

Several witnesses who saw the accident reported on the actual weather conditions at the time. The engineering sub-contractors reported that the weather was 'clear, sunny and fine with good visibility, enough to see the Lake District hills'. One witness, an experienced balloon pilot, described the weather as 'bright conditions with approximately 30 km visibility and broken cloud at about 3,500 feet'.

1.8   Aids to navigation

Not applicable.

1.9   Communications

The helicopter pilot maintained routine radio contact with ATC units en route on Very High Frequency (VHF) frequencies. On departure from Blackpool Air Traffic Zone (ATZ) the controller advised the pilot that a Lower Airspace Radar Service (LARS) was available from Warton Radar. One minute later the pilot contacted Warton Approach Radar, on 124.45 MHz, stating that he was 'JUST OUTBOUND FROM BLACKPOOL RESUMING THE LOW LEVEL PIPELINE THREE HUNDRED AT INSKIP...WE'LL BE RESUMING NORTHBOUND TRACK BACK TOWARDS EDINBURGH'. By 1024 hrs the pilot reported to Warton that he was 'ON THE PIPELINE WORKING OUR WAY NORTHBOUND'. The controller replied 'THANK YOU, KEEP A GOOD LOOKOUT'. At 1041 hrs the pilot made an attempt to communicate with Warton which was unsuccessful, probably because of his low altitude and so he changed to the London Flight Information frequency of 134.7 MHz. No transmissions from the pilot were recorded on this frequency.

The Tornado crew maintained routine radio contact where possible with Military Air Traffic Control Units on Ultra High Frequency (UHF) channels throughout their transit flight to the east coast bombing ranges. Whilst operating as a pair the Tornados maintained contact with each other on their common air-to-air UHF frequency, changing to the appropriate airfield frequency only as they transited through various Military Air Traffic Zones (MATZ).

1.10   Aerodrome information

Not applicable.

1.11   Flight recorders

1.11.1   Replay of Flight Recorders

There was no Cockpit Voice Recorder or Flight Data Recorder fitted to the JetRanger and neither was required to be fitted. The Tornado carried a Sperry SCR200 Accident Data Recorder (ADR) with combined voice and data recordings consisting of one track of audio information and 3 tracks of flight data each of one hour duration. The track allocation was as follows:

Channel 1	Audio
Channel 2	Data #1
Channel 3	Data #2
Channel 4	Data #3

The ADR was replayed by the Aircraft & Armament Evaluation Establishment at Boscombe Down and a copy of the audio and flight data was passed to the AAIB.

The method of operation of the recorder results in the most recently recorded data track being synchronised to the audio. Data is recorded in a one second frame where a status word is located at the start of each second followed by 127 data words; the position of the collision can therefore be determined accurately in relation to the recorded data. The collision occurred at 1049 hrs UTC exactly (to within ±2 seconds, timing related to the ATC tapes). At this point there was an audible bang, which was probably the sound of initial impact of the Tornado with the JetRanger. There was no indication from either crew on the audio track that they had seen the JetRanger before or after the collision.

1.11.2   Interpretation of Data

Appendix A Figure 1 shows selected parameters from the ADR, beginning 40 seconds before the collision. The Tornado was on a compass heading of 297°, at 455 kt airspeed and at a recorded barometric altitude of between 400 and 500 feet, based on 1,013 mb, which corresponds to between 510 and 610 feet above mean sea level. The resolution of the barometric altitude is 128 feet.

About 30 seconds before impact the Tornado rolled to the right onto a heading of 304°, and then left gradually onto 301°. After impact the Tornado pitched up and climbed as indicated by the radio height.

Appendix A Figure 2 shows a expanded plot of these parameters in the area of the impact at 1049 hrs UTC. At 5 seconds before impact the Tornado rolled from 22° left wing down to an approximate wings level attitude just prior to the collision. The roll continued and reached 6.4° right wing down at impact, with a pitch attitude of 2.6° nose up. The compass heading was 303°, the recorded radio height was 381 feet. The pitot/static information was lost after impact as the probe was damaged. The right-hand engine began to run down after the collision as shown by the recording of the HP rotor speed.

The ground track of the Tornado was derived from the recorded data assuming a wind of 300°/7 kt. The exact position of the collision was not known, but from the distribution of the wreckage on the ground an approximate position for the collision is marked on Appendix A Figure 3, which also shows the estimated track of the Tornado up to that point and the ground contours in the area. The position on the ground where most of the wreckage from the JetRanger landed is also shown. Appendix A Figure 4 shows this in a three-dimensional view, with height calculated from the Radio Height corrected for the ground level below the estimated track.

1.12   Wreckage and impact information

1.12.1   Helicopter

The wreckage of the helicopter lay in the yard of Dove House farm at map reference SD 541818, some 10 metres from outbuildings. Most of the aircraft was in this one location apart from the tail boom approximately aft of the horizontal stabiliser which was not in evidence. The aircraft had descended at a high rate almost vertically into the ground while rolled slightly to the right in a level pitch attitude. The tail boom had fallen across a hedgerow and thus the in-flight damage was not overlaid by ground impact disruption. The relative lack of damage to the main rotor blades indicated that they had very little rotational energy at impact.

Most of the missing structure was located approximately 130 metres to the south of the main wreckage in a trail of some 250 metres length running roughly south east/north west. Virtually all the light airframe structure was here together with the tail rotor blades. There was no sign of the heavier mechanical parts such as the tail rotor gearbox, hub or blade grips. Later examination of the damage to the Tornado resulted in recovery of a substantial proportion of the gearbox (see following paragraph), and the tail rotor shaft with about 30% of the crown gearwheel was found some days later about 4 miles further along the track of the Tornado. The blade grips and hub were not found but may have been in the canal or rough uncultivated ground to the west of the identified wreckage trail.

The HISL selector switch was found in the 'HISL white' position. Since this is an unguarded switch it is not certain that this was a pre-impact position but it is consistent with the expected selection. During the course of the subsequent examination at the AAIB at Farnborough it was possible to check the operation of the HISL by applying power to the circuit and it was found to operate normally in both the white and red selections. The smaller strobe lights fitted to the extremities of the horizontal stabilisers had been broken by impact but their electronic unit housed in the fuselage was serviceable.

Although most of the wreckage found at the site was from the helicopter, some debris from the Tornado was found amongst the wreckage trail. There were identifiable pieces of the plastic radome and sections of skin panel from the right engine intake, including the navigation light fitted in this location.

1.12.2   Tornado

The Tornado was examined at the BAe factory at Warton, Lancashire. The most obvious sign of impact with the helicopter was the badly damaged radome which had been disrupted along its upper right side and the pitot probe was bent downwards. Pieces of the helicopter tail rotor gearbox mounting structure and the casing itself were found embedded in the radar components in this area.

A fairing over the refuelling probe was torn and there was a heavy scrape on the right side windscreen and frame. Further aft there were panels torn out of the outer skin of the right engine intake lip where an object appeared to have burst through from the inside. These were the skin panels found at the accident site. There were also heavy impacts on the right wing inboard leading edge slats and 'nib' fairing with a heavy gouge on the inboard pylon. The airframe had received many more minor scratches and impacts from light debris.

The most serious damage had resulted from debris that had been ingested into the right engine some of which had destroyed all the stages of the compressor. Much of the IP and HP compressor and the turbine section had burnt away. Some of this debris had been ejected forwards after contact with the LP1 compressor blades and had punched a hole in the intake duct just forward of the engine front face.

All the debris recovered from the engine and from behind the intake duct comprised parts of the helicopter tail rotor gearbox and the majority of this component was thus accounted for.

1.12.3.   Collision parameters

First contact was made with the Tornado pitot probe piercing the relatively light fairing around the helicopter tail rotor gearbox. The gearbox had torn open the radome and struck its aft lip known as 'the skirt'. This latter impact detached and disrupted the gearbox and tail rotor, the heavy components of which were then ingested into the right engine intake. It would appear that some substantial parts, possibly the blade grips, burst through the side of the intake whilst most of the gearbox itself was ingested by the engine. The helicopter's light vertical fin structure had wrapped around the upper fuselage of the Tornado, striking the canopy.

As the impact sequence progressed the helicopter tailboom, already truncated with the loss of the tail rotor gearbox, received a further impact from the right wing leading edge of the Tornado, removing more of its structure and damaging the horizontal stabiliser. The helicopter's pitch attitude was level and the two aircraft were at right angles to each other.

With the light northwesterly wind at the time of the accident and the low height at which the collision occurred, it was concluded that the actual point of collision was approximately above the centre of the wreckage trail (map reference SD 540816), with lighter debris being blown back towards the south east and heavier items being thrown to the north west.

1.13   **Medical and pathological information**

A post-mortem and toxicological examination was carried out on the pilot of the JetRanger. No evidence was found of medical factors which might have caused or contributed to the accident.

The pilot and navigator of the Tornado were interviewed by the Deputy Senior Medical Officer of RAF Bruggen on the day after the accident. Both had had a good night's rest before the flight and showed no signs of being unwell within the preceding 24 hours.

1.14　Fire

Although the fuel tank of the helicopter was ruptured on impact with the ground there was no fire. The right engine of the Tornado suffered a titanium fire but this extinguished itself moments after the collision.

1.15　Survival aspects

A police officer who witnessed the accident alerted the emergency services shortly after 1049 hrs and they arrived on the scene at 1109 hrs to find that the pilot and observer had sustained fatal injuries on impact with the ground.

The decelerative forces experienced by the pilot and observer of the JetRanger were well beyond human tolerance. The seat belt and diagonal torso strap of the pilot remained intact although there was gross distortion of the cabin area. The lap portion of the observer's harness became detached at the outboard end due to airframe distortion on impact.

1.16　Tests and research

1.16.1　Visual detection and collision recognition

In order to assess the probability of detection in the circumstances of this accident, advice was sought from the Principal Psychologist of the Institute of Aviation Medicine (IAM). His report, which is at Appendix B, concludes that the circumstances of this accident illuminate the general problem of collision avoidance. Given the difficulty of detecting small aircraft, a fast jet (FJ) pilot needs to sweep his forward sector about every five seconds (including head movements to clear canopy obstructions) in order to have a reasonable chance of avoiding conflicts. This is difficult enough without the other demands on his attention at low level including navigation, terrain avoidance, station keeping and aircraft systems management. The pilot of a slow moving aircraft needs to scan an even wider area.

Analysis of the contour map and the Tornado ADR data indicate that the relief features of Farleton Knott and Farleton Fell did not obscure either pilot's view of the other aircraft for a significant time before the collision. The estimated probability of the Tornado detecting the JetRanger indicates that the latter was effectively invisible until about 17 seconds before the collision. However, the cumulative probability of detection was minimal until about five seconds from impact. At impact minus 7 to 5 seconds the probability of detection would rise sharply; as long as obscuration did not play a part. The Tornado, having better contrast and being a larger target, would have been in principle somewhat more detectable.

It is possible to enhance the conspicuity of aircraft by a suitable choice of paint scheme and by the addition of sufficiently bright lights. Lights considerably brighter than the existing HISLs, which are of at least 2,000 candela (cd), are currently being considered. Collision warning systems would enhance the effectiveness of visual lookout, particularly if fitted to civil as well as military aircraft. These are, however, unlikely to prove a complete solution unless employed in combination with improvements in aircraft conspicuity.

1.16.2   Summary of Australian Bureau of Air Safety Investigation research report

Investigations carried out by the Australian Bureau of Air Safety Investigation (BASI) into mid-air collisions that occurred in Australia in the late 1980's, drew attention to the deficiencies of the 'see-and-avoid' concept for air traffic separation. As a consequence, the BASI made an evaluation of the practicality of the 'see-and-avoid' principle in controlled and uncontrolled airspace. The report on their research, which was published in April 1991, is at Appendix C. It refers to international research of this problem and highlights concisely some serious limitations of the 'see-and-avoid' principle.

While 'see-and-avoid' undoubtedly prevents many collisions, the principle is far from reliable. Numerous limitations, including those of the human visual system, the demands of cockpit tasks, and various physical and environmental conditions combine to make 'see-and-avoid' an uncertain method of traffic separation. Cockpit workload and other factors reduce the time that pilots spend in traffic scans. However, even when pilots are looking out, there is no guarantee that other aircraft will be sighted. Most cockpit windscreen configurations severely limit the view available to the pilot which is frequently interrupted by obstructions such as window-posts which totally obscure some parts of the view and make other areas visible to only one eye. Window posts, windscreen crazing and dirt can act as 'focal traps' and cause the pilot to focus involuntarily at a very short distance even when attempting to scan for traffic. Direct glare from the sun and veiling glare reflected from windscreens can effectively mask some areas of the view.

Visual scanning involves moving the eyes in order to bring successive areas of the visual field onto the small area of sharp vision in the centre of the eye. The process is frequently unsystematic and may leave large areas of the field of view unsearched. The contrast between an aircraft and its background can be significantly reduced by atmospheric effects, even in conditions of good visibility.

An approaching aircraft, in many cases, presents a very small visual angle until a short time before impact. Even when an approaching aircraft has been sighted, there is no guarantee that evasive action will be successful. It takes a significant amount of time to recognise and respond to a collision threat and an inappropriate evasive manoeuvre may serve to increase rather than decrease the chance of a collision.

The BASI report concluded that unalerted 'see-and-avoid' had a limited place as a last resort means of traffic separation at low closing speeds but was not sufficiently reliable to warrant a greater role in the air traffic system. It was considered that many of the limitations of 'see-and-avoid' were associated with physical limits to human perception, however there was some scope to improve the effectiveness of 'see-and-avoid' in other areas such as conspicuity and improved anti-collision lights.

1.16.3   Collision Warning System

To assist in the deconfliction of military aircraft involved in high speed low level training operations the Ministry of Defence (MOD) are funding development of an airborne electronic Collision Warning System (CWS). It is expected that CWS will also provide collision warning information on civil aircraft with suitable transponding equipment.

An aircraft installed system interrogates other aircraft which are equipped with ATC transponders using mode 'A' or 'C'. The specification calls for its use in low-level operations only, detecting potential threats out to a range of 20 nm, 60° either side, 10° below and 20° above the nose of the aircraft. The ability to interrogate five targets simultaneously is specified and the system should be able to deal with closure rates of up to 1,000 kt with an accuracy of bearing information in the order of ± 15°. By acquiring range and bearing information the system will calculate a collision threat in time and distance. This will produce two types of threat alert. Type 1 will give a warning of closing traffic inside 15 seconds to collision. Type 2 will give a warning of closing traffic inside 5 seconds to collision, and warning of 'pop-up' traffic inside 2 nm. Having been alerted to the threat the pilot will take the necessary action to avoid a collision.

The CWS requirement is currently at the stage of a Technology Demonstrator Programme (TDP) involving flight trials of the equipment throughout most of 1994. A progress report is to be issued in December 1994. The results of the TDP, along with policy and economic considerations, will determine the future of the programme.

A civil system known as the Traffic Alerting and Collision Avoidance System (TCAS), which is already in use and is mandatory equipment in some large civil aircraft operating in certain ATC environments, is considered unsuitable for military FJ operations. It resolves conflictions by advising manoeuvres in the vertical plane and this would be inappropriate at low level.

1.16.4   Electronic strobe detection

Just as HISLs and other lights are designed to enhance conspicuity so pilots' ability to detect such lights visually may be augmented by the use of an electronic detection device. A study had been funded by the CAA to review the possibilities offered by modern optical components to detect Xenon strobe lights fitted on military and many private aircraft [4]. The type of system envisaged would be two sensors, probably installed above and below the fuselage to provide the maximum field of view, linked to a display/audio warning in the cockpit. Initial results indicate that it may be feasible to develop a practical system using innovative design at a cost that might be attractive even to light aircraft operators and progress reports are awaited.

1.17   Additional information

1.17.1   Military low flying

The RAF has a continuing requirement to train its pilots in the low level reconnaissance and attack roles. Before 1976 specific areas within the UK were designated as areas available for military low flying. These areas were joined by designated low flying corridors known as link routes, however, since 1979 the whole of the UK is in principle open to low flying but in practice environmental and safety restrictions halve the airspace available. Conurbation and the airspace designated for flights which are conducted under positive ATC control at all times are excluded. For administrative convenience, the country is now divided into 19 Low Flying Areas (LFA), not evidently linked to any geographical divisions on the ground.

In the UK, military FJs are considered to be low flying when they are less than 2,000 feet from the ground, water or any object except another aircraft flying in the same formation. The lowest height at which a military jet is normally permitted to fly is 250 feet MSD. Foreign military aircraft are subject to a policy of 'reciprocity' under which they are not allowed to fly in the UK at a lower height than applies to RAF aircraft in the country concerned. For example German aircraft may not operate in the UK below their national limit of

---

[4]   CAA Project Code: No 9.3; Title: Conspicuity; Objectives: Improved visibiltiy of airborne hazards.

1,000 feet agl which also applies to RAF aircraft operating in Germany. Low flying by foreign aircraft accounts for less than 2% of the total activity in the UK Low Flying System.

About 80% of FJ low flying training takes place between 250 and 500 feet MSD and is carried out on weekdays, during daylight and in good weather. Except in the Highland Restricted Area, which is set aside on a regular basis for low flying in limited visibility using terrain following radar, all low flying by day is in Visual Meteorological Conditions (VMC), that is pilots must be able to fly by visual reference to the ground. Details of Military Low Flying in the UK are published in UK Aeronautical Information Circular (AIC) -AIC 89/1993 (Yellow 107) and in the RAC Section of the UK Aeronautical Information Publication (AIP). Chart RAC 5-0-1.1 is a chart showing Areas of Intense Aerial Activity (AAIA), Aerial Tactics Areas (ATA) and detail of the Military Low Flying System. It is intended that this chart will include the flow structure which was recommended in Aircraft Accident Report (AAR) 2/92 on the mid-air collision at Carno, Powys in August 1991 [5].

Nearly all low flying sorties are required to be planned and then notified to a central co-ordinating authority, normally the London Air Traffic Control Centre (Military) Tactical Booking Cell (TBC) at West Drayton. This centre co-ordinates military low flying sorties and also provides co-ordination with civil aircraft whose flights have been notified in accordance with the Civil Aircraft Notification Procedures (CANP) and Pipeline inspection Notification System (PINS) (see paragraph 1.17.3).

The organisation and control of military low flying and its co-ordination with civil aviation is under constant review and the TBC anticipate the use of a new Automated Low Flying Enquiry and Notification System (ALFENS). This computerised system will speed up communications and provide up to date information on the UK low flying system at all FJ operating bases. It is expected to become operational in Spring 1995.

1.17 2   Civil low flying

Aircraft are not normally permitted to fly closer than 500 feet to any person, vessel, vehicle or structure [6]. In order to operate to a height as low as 300 feet agl, the helicopter operator had been granted by the CAA an exemption to the normal rules. This exemption permitted helicopter flights down to 300 feet agl when within a horizontal distance of 300 feet from the pipelines to be inspected.

---

5   AAR 2/92 Recommendation 92-8

6   Article 69 of the Air Navigation Order 1989 Rules of The Air Regulations 1991 Section II para 5 (1) (e)

Typically such exemptions require that helicopters are to be fitted with a white HISL of at least 2,000 cd intensity. The JetRanger was fitted with a red/white HISL which was selected on 'HISL WHITE' at the time of the accident. After the accident, on 28 September 1993, the AAIB made a recommendation that the CAA should circulate a notice to AOC [7] holders involved in aerial surveys recommending that where practical they operate in the height band 500 feet to 700 feet thus providing a degree of vertical separation from high speed low flying military aircraft which will generally operate below 500 feet. [Recommendation 93-47].

On 17 August 1993 the CAA (Flight Operations Inspectorate) wrote to all helicopter AOC holders describing additional safety measures proposed as a result of this accident. The letter stated:

> '.....with effect from commencement of operations on 23 August 1993, pipe-line inspections will be flown in the height bracket 500-700 feet above ground level, with 600 feet agl optimum. The RAF have confirmed that 80% of their fast jet low flying traffic will pass below 500 feet, thus in theory a measure of vertical separation for safety purposes will have been established. It is appreciated that pilots of pipe-line patrol helicopters will still have to descend below 500 feet for closer inspection of faults and so on: this practice will continue to be authorised by an easement from Rule 5 (1) (e) obtainable from this inspectorate. Pilots will have to exercise normal airmanship in carrying out a conscientious clearing turn prior to any descent into the possible military operating height band, and should return to their 600 feet as rapidly as possible.'

The letter also gave advance notice of an AIC which was published on 21 October 1993 confirming these arrangement and introducing the new procedure of PINS (see paragraph 1.17.3 below). The CAA also publishes a Safety Sense Leaflet on Collision Avoidance which gives advice to civil pilots, including advice on correct scanning techniques.

1.17.3   Notification Procedures (CANP and PINS)

Although military aircraft are considered to be low flying when they are below 2,000 feet agl, it is not practicable to disseminate information on all civil aircraft operating at that height or below. The greatest risk of collision exists at or below 500 feet agl where much of the low level military operations take place. Since 1974, following a collision between an RAF Phantom FJ and a Piper Pawnee crop spraying aircraft, the system of Low Level Civil Aircraft Notification Procedure (CANP) has been available to civil operators. This gives civil aircraft

---

7   Air Operators Certificate required for public transport undertakings

engaged in aerial work within 2 miles of a datum and for a duration in excess of 20 minutes operating below 1,000 feet agl the opportunity to notify their presence to military operators who will then arrange to avoid the notified area. The procedure, which is voluntary, is fully described in the United Kingdom Air Pilot (UK AIP), Rules of the Air and Air Traffic Services (RAC) 3-10-1. Commercial agricultural aviation operators are required to use CANP, whenever appropriate, under the terms of their Operations Manuals and Aerial Application Certificates.

Pipeline and power line inspection flights by helicopters were originally included in this procedure but there was considerable difficulty in providing, at the necessary notice, sufficiently accurate times and positions for aerial survey activities. Following a trial by the principal operator at the time, and with the full agreement of the British Helicopter Advisory Board (BHAB), such inspection flights were excluded from the system in 1984.

After the accident AAIB Recommendation 93-48 was made on 28 September 1993 and was that:

> 'The Civil Aviation Authority should introduce a system of area notification of information to military crews involved in low flying training that provides the timely distribution on civil aerial activity relating to the surveying of pipelines in the UK.'

In response it was agreed by CAA (NATS - Airspace Policy) and the operators of aerial survey flights that a system of notification such as CANP was essential (refer to AAIB Safety Recommendation 93-48 and AIC 156/1993 (Yellow 126)). A new procedure to cater for the particular needs of pipeline inspection flights was devised. Known as the Pipeline Inspection Notification System (PINS), details of the system are published in an Aeronautical Information Circular (AIC) which is reproduced at Appendix D.

Recommendation 93-49 was also made on 28 September 1993 and was that:

> 'The Ministry of Defence (RAF), in consultation with the Health and Safety Executive and the known energy providers, should obtain for crews involved in low level flying training suitable briefing material on the location and routes of the major pipelines within the UK. The briefing material should include any known frequency of routine inspections with provision for any variations to be notified by the operators.'

Since the accident this briefing material has been provided by MOD.

1.17.4   Volume of aerial survey flights

An estimate of pipeline survey flights, which are conducted on a random weekly or fortnightly basis and subject to suitable weather conditions, gives a maximum of 147 hours per week flown by a maximum of 13 helicopters. Other statistics indicate an annual total of pipeline inspection flights of some 6,000 hours.

1.17.5   Volume of military low flying

The following table shows estimated number of low flying sorties flown during the period 1987 to 92:

Year:	1987	1988	1989	1990	1991	1992
Sorties:	146,500	151,000	144,000	141,000	127,400	131,450

Of these totals about two thirds were flights by FJs [8] and one third other aircraft including helicopters. On any week day there may be as many as 600 military low flying sorties planned. On 14 October 1991 HM Government announced that, due to proposed changes in the structure of the armed forces, low flying flights over the UK by military jets would be progressively reduced by about 30% on the 1988 baseline figures over the following three years.

1.17.6   Mid-air collision statistics

The database maintained by the Safety Data Analysis Unit of the Safety Regulation Group, CAA, includes details of mid-air collisions involving UK civil powered light aircraft (see Appendix E). From May 1977 until June 1993 there have been 30 mid-air collisions in UK airspace. In these there were 26 fatalities with no injuries to persons on the ground.

Excluding collisions in the circuit, formation aerobatics, air-to-air photography and other close proximity manoeuvres, there were only seven random collisions in the UK open FIR. Three of these occurred between military and civil aircraft. These were:

a. 29 February 1984 - USAF A10 / Cessna 152, Hardwick, Norfolk.

b. 29 August 1991 - RAF Jaguar T2A / Cessna 152, Carno, Wales.

c. 23 June 1993 - RAF Tornado GR1 / Agusta Bell 206B JetRanger III, Farleton Knott, near Kendal, Cumbria.

---

8   A Fast Jet is defined as an aircraft whose major portion of flight is in excess of 300 kt IAS.

The remaining four involved civil aircraft only and occurred between 1,800 and 3,300 feet.

1.17.7   Airmiss statistics

Whenever an airmiss is reported by one or both of the pilots involved, the circumstances are investigated by the Joint Airmiss Section (JAS), a section of NATS which is a joint civil/military air traffic organisation. Once the evidence has been assembled by JAS it is discussed by the Joint Airmiss Working Group (JAWG) who assess the degree of risk inherent in each occurrence. The degree of risk is assessed in accordance with the International Civil Aviation Organisation (ICAO) guide lines and categorised as follows:

Category 'A' - Actual risk of collision

Category 'B' - Possible risk of collision

Category 'C' - Other reports with no assessed risk of collision

JAS maintains a data base of all airmisses and, after the JAWG assessment, each airmiss is coded under a wide range of parameters including aircraft types, the location and geometry of the incidents, passing distance, degree of risk and cause. The database was interrogated to provide details of all airmisses during a three year period between low flying military and civil GA aircraft at 2,000 feet and below. The figures for 1990 are for 6 months from June to December. The figures for 1993 are for 6 months from January to June. The statistics are for Category 'A' and 'B' risks only.

Year	1990 (6 months)	1991	1992	1993 (6 months)	Total
Category 'A'	5	5	3	0	13
Category 'B'	6	19	11	6	42

1.17.8   Relevant legislation

1.17.8.1   The Rules of the Air Regulations 1991

The Rules of the Air Regulations 1991 are published in full in Section 2 of the Air Navigation Order (ANO) 1989. The following extracts are pertinent to this investigation:

24

'Low Flying

5 (1) Subject to the provisions of paragraphs (2) and (3):

(b) A helicopter shall not fly below such height as would enable it to alight without danger to persons or property on the surface, in the event of failure of a power unit.

(e) An aircraft shall not fly closer than 500 feet to any person, vessel, vehicle or structure.

Rules for avoiding aerial collisions

17 (1) General

(a) Notwithstanding that the flight is being made with air traffic control clearance it shall remain the duty of the commander of an aircraft to take all possible measures to ensure that his aircraft does not collide with another aircraft.

(b) An aircraft shall not be flown in such proximity to other aircraft as to create a danger of collision

(2) Converging

(b) ....when two aircraft are converging in the air at approximately the same altitude, the aircraft which has the other on its right shall give way:

(3) Approaching head-on

When two aircraft are approaching head-on or approximately so in the air and there is a danger of collision, each shall alter its course to the right.

Speed Limitation

23 (1) Subject to paragraph (3), an aircraft shall not fly below flight level 100 at a speed which according to its airspeed indicator is more than 250 knots unless it is flying in accordance with the terms of a written permission of the Authority.'

1.17.8.2 Military Flying Regulations

Military Flying Regulations (Second Edition April 1992) are published for official use in a Joint Service Publication (JSP) No 318. The following entry appears in the joint regulations section Chapter 053 paragraph 05304:

'2. Military aircraft are to conform to the civil national ATC system of all foreign countries over which they fly. In the UK, the system of air traffic control is based on a joint civil/military scheme in which the military aviation authorities observe such ICAO regulations as have been accepted by the Civil Aviation Authority, provided they do not impair the operational freedom of military aircraft.'

Furthermore the Air Navigation Order Part VIII, Control of Air traffic, Article 69 paragraph 3 states:

'(3)   It shall be lawful for the Rules of the Air to be departed from to the extent necessary:

(a)   for avoiding immediate danger

(b)   for complying with the law of any country other than the United Kingdom within which the aircraft then is; or

(c)   for complying with Military Flying Regulations (Joint Service Publication 318) or Flying Orders to Contractors (Aviation Publication 67) issued by the Secretary of State in relation to an aircraft of which the commander is acting as such in the course of his duty as a member of any of Her Majesty's naval, military or air forces.'

In addition to JSP 318 regulations, Service pilots fly to detailed rules promulgated in the UK Military Low Flying Handbook (LFHB).

1.18   New investigation techniques

None.

2   Analysis

2.1   The collision

The collision between the high speed low flying military jet and the slow speed
low flying civil helicopter occurred at a height of about 380 feet agl in
uncontrolled airspace where both aircraft were being operated in accordance with
their relevant regulations. It is clear from the Tornado crew's recollection that
they had not sighted the JetRanger; indeed they were unaware of the collision
until after they had landed and examined the damage sustained by their aircraft. It
is highly unlikely that the JetRanger pilot saw the Tornado since he had just
completed a left-hand orbit before rolling onto a northerly heading. The pilot
therefore would have been looking initially to his left and then concentrating on
the next part of his route which was almost at right angles to the Tornado's track.
Strict interpretation of the Rules of the Air required the JetRanger to give way to
the Tornado because the latter aircraft was on the JetRanger's right. Moments
before, however, the aircraft had been head on to each other requiring both to
give way. In either case a sighting was an essential pre-requisite for avoidance.
Even if the JetRanger pilot had seen the Tornado at a late stage his speed of
horizontal manoeuvre may have been too slow to move out of the way, although a
rapid descent may have been possible. Furthermore, with such a rapidly
changing spatial relationship, consideration of the 'right of way' rules is quite
inappropriate.

The tragedy was compounded by the loss of control of the helicopter after it had
been struck by the Tornado. Whilst the collision was probably catastrophic, there
may have been a slight chance for the JetRanger pilot to cope with the loss of his
tail rotor. Routine training and proficiency checks include the simulation of loss
of tail rotor thrust and handling techniques are available to permit a safe landing
under such conditions. In this case, however, the complete tail rotor assembly
and vertical stabiliser had been severed in the collision and this would have
significantly affected the helicopter's centre of gravity. This factor, combined
with the pilot's shock and disorientation due to the initial rotations in yaw, most
likely contributed to the ultimate loss of control.

2.2   See-and-avoid

Primary reliance on the principle of 'see-and-avoid' for separation, with its
acknowledged limitations, is a major contribution to the risk of collision. Military
low flying training is an essential feature of UK national defence policy and
requires constant practise by military pilots. Under existing arrangements this
requires the use of major portions of the UK low level airspace. Civil aviation
has an equal right and need to use the same airspace and, because of a gross

incompatibility in operational modes, civil and military airspace users constitute a risk to each other. However, such a risk can be set in the context of many natural hazards which may be encountered by both military and civil aircraft. For example turbulence, thunderstorms, freezing rain, high tension cables, tall aerial masts and cloud covered high ground are frequently encountered. Most of these are either predictable or documented and publicised so that a pilot may, by careful briefing, meticulous planning and prudent flying, avoid or reduce the hazards. However, the risk posed by a FJ / light aircraft confliction is less easily foreseen and therefore it cannot be countered simply by using the same methods as those employed against natural hazards. Additional help is required by using technology such as a Collision Warning System (CWS) and, where available, ATC information in order to increase traffic awareness and hence reduce further the risks involved.

The only separation criteria in force at the time of the Tornado/JetRanger collision were that both pilots were responsible for their own collision avoidance using the 'see-and-avoid' principle. There was no other air traffic control or information service being provided. There was no technical system available to alert either crew to the proximity of other aircraft, even the Tornado's electronic sensors are not designed to do this. The collision was clear evidence that, in this situation, the 'see and avoid' principle had failed. It is therefore questionable as to whether it is an appropriate method for the deconfliction of such incompatible users of the low level airspace.

Failure in the 'see-and-avoid' principle was a feature of the three other collisions between FJs and civil light aircraft which have occurred since 1976, the previous one having occurred in August 1991. They all occurred because one or both pilot's failed to 'see-and-avoid' the collision. Furthermore, in all cases the type of operation did not allow total concentration on collision avoidance which is an essential prerequisite of 'see-and-avoid'. In the case of this accident the JetRanger pilot was performing an observation task on a pipeline and the Tornado pilot was looking for his leader. In the case of the Carno collision in August 1991, the Cessna pilot was engaged in aerial photography while the Jaguar crew were identifying a particular object on the ground. In the case of the 1984 collision between an A10 and a Cessna 152, the Cessna pilot was engaged on a student qualifying navigation exercise and the A10 pilot was selecting an RT frequency which required him to look inside the cockpit. In every case there were valid reasons for less than complete attention to the 'see-and-avoid' task.

Also, during the year of this accident, there were six reported airmisses involving military FJs and civil light aircraft. They were all assessed by JAWG as Category 'B' *i.e.* a possible risk of collision. In some cases a very late sighting had enabled an avoiding manoeuvre to be executed but the airmisses nevertheless highlight the limitations of 'see-and-avoid'. Although the collisions and airmisses just mentioned represent a small statistical sample, it is clear that the chance of another collision under the existing system of low flying in the UK, relying as it does so heavily on the principle of 'see and avoid', remains finite.

It is therefore recommended that the Ministry of Defence should commission an operational analysis of FJ low flying training in the UK to determine whether the use of 'see-and-avoid' as the primary means of collision avoidance is satisfactory from the point of view of flight safety. [Recommendation 94-1]

2.3   Conflicting interests of low level airspace users

Whereas military aircraft are deemed to be low flying when below 2,000 feet agl, civil aircraft are bound by the 'Low Flying' rules of The Rules of the Air Regulations 1991 which for all practical purposes mean that low flying is deemed to occur below 500 feet agl. This analysis will concentrate on the lower height band (below 500 feet) because that is where most of the FJ activity takes place. Nevertheless the definition of 'low level airspace' includes the height band from ground level to 2,000 feet and the problems of deconflicting civil and military traffic should be considered in this broader height band. There is no doubt that the mix of FJ and civil aircraft in the low level airspace constitutes a risk to all who use it.

National policy governing civil and military aviation permits joint use of the low level airspace and has been in existence for many years. Any exclusivity of use would require legislation and this investigation has noted the views of the House of Commons Select Committee on Defence on the subject of military low flying [9] which considered, amongst other matters, the conflicting interests of FJ and civil aircraft. The safety problem stems from the incompatibility of the joint airspace users, both of whom are entitled under UK law to exercise their respective privileges equally. The increase in FJ capability in terms of speed and navigational accuracy combined with their requirement for large training areas has, in recent years, widened the gulf of incompatibility with slower flying aerial work and GA aircraft. There is serious concern by those responsible for the safety regulation of civil aviation that the continuing risk of collision merits more positive steps towards deconfliction.

---

9   House of Commons Defence Committee report printed on 28 March 1990.

There are four main areas in which improvements may be considered. They are:

a.   physical separation of incompatible airspace users by time and space and;

b.   procedural deconfliction and;

c.   technological assistance for visual acquisition and recognition times and;

d.   common radio communication in the low level airspace.

2.4   Separation of civil and military traffic in the low level airspace

Military aircraft are by far the major users of the low level airspace. There are some 600 sorties each weekday. The current annual figure of some 120,000 military low flying sorties far outweighs the annual total of aerial survey flights (6,000 hours pipeline and 4,000 hours power line). Within the low level airspace up to 2,000 feet, civil aircraft activity increases considerably taking account of a large amount of GA flying. Total GA activity in the UK has been estimated as 2 million hours per year. Unrefined statistics such as these may give a misleading impression but what is clear is that military aircraft are the majority users of the low level airspace below 500 feet and it is that height band that is most relevant to this accident.

Military aircraft operating in the low level airspace are not required to conform to the same regulations applying to civil aircraft (see paragraphs 1.17.1 and 1.17.2). Military regulations are contained in JSP 318 and in the UK LFHB. Civil regulations are found in the Air Navigation Order. Whereas military aircraft will observe ICAO and national regulations, except where operational requirements dictate otherwise, a lack of common regulations for users of the low level airspace must contribute to the risk of collision. This is most manifest in the different airspeeds which are permitted. Although civil aircraft are limited to speeds less than 250 kt when operating below FL100 (10,000 feet on the standard altimeter setting) in practise very few of the civil aircraft operating in the open FIR and even fewer operating below 1,000 feet can be described as high speed. The majority of high performance civil aircraft operate in controlled airspace where traffic is under positive control and collision avoidance is more assured. This means that there is an even greater speed discrepancy between FJ and civil aircraft at low level particularly since the probability of detection is inversely proportional to closing speeds.

Exclusivity of use of the low level airspace, however desirable, is unlikely to be approved for either military or civil users. It would be politically unacceptable to deny the open FIR to one or other of the legitimate users although mutual programming of activity might be considered. For example there is increased GA traffic at weekends and a corresponding decrease in military flying. To formalise a programme of exclusive use of the low flying areas would need to account for bad weather and might prejudice the flexibility of all the current low level airspace users. Thus incompatibility of FJ and GA remains as the major air safety problem but there are certain palliative measures, which taken together, could reduce the risks of collision.

2.4.1.   Lateral separation - Low Flying System

In the past, military low flying in the UK has been confined to recognised low flying areas with a system of low level link routes permitting transit from one to the other. This system was discontinued in 1979 since the RAF had concluded that the link route and area system then in force could only safely accommodate some 80,000 low flying sorties per year. Calculations showed that, when the full complement of Tornado aircraft entered service, there would be a need for some 150,000 sorties a year. The old system could not cope with these numbers and thus, primarily for reasons of safety, the modern UK Low Flying System (UKLFS) was introduced. The actual area available for low flying is much restricted by large urban areas, controlled airspace and other areas which must be avoided. Although the previous low flying system was superseded, the actual gain in available area would appear to have been minimal. One undesirable feature of the low level link routes was that it tended to concentrate low flying over specific areas which gave rise to understandable complaints from residents living beneath the affected areas. By adopting a somewhat more free traffic pattern and by using, in theory, the whole country these complaints were diluted. One highly desirable feature of the link routes was that other airspace users could be much more certain about the chances of encountering low flying military aircraft in the vicinity of the routes than they could be in the open airspace. This required them to know the location of the low level routes and, although only published on military low flying charts, there was widespread civilian knowledge of the routes.

Following the collision between an RAF Jaguar and Cessna 152 near Carno, Powys in August 1991, it was recommended in AAR 2/92 that military flow directional arrows should be published on civil aeronautical charts.[10] These flow direction arrows were practically the successors to the low level link routes and came about partly as a result of the natural constrictions placed on low flying by numerous obstructions such as urban areas, other airspace, avoidance and sensitive areas and partly as a safety measure introduced to the military low flying system so that all its users could be aware of 'choke points' and to flow through

---

[10]   AAR 2/92 Recommendation 92-8.

31

them in a single specified direction. Unfortunately, the implementation of the AAIB recommendation resulted in this information being published in the UK AIP as an addition to an existing small scale chart showing the military low flying system in the UK. It has not appeared, as the recommendation intended, on the topographical charts most commonly used by civil pilots and which are instantly available in the cockpit. Reluctance to further clutter a chart which already contains a mass of useful information was given as a reason for using the AIP as the method of promulgation.

A more recent review of the UKLFS by MOD in 1991/2 re-examined the question of link routes and training areas. Its re-introduction was rejected primarily on safety grounds. The majority of military low flying involves independent flows which are highly localised and are designed to prevent military only conflictions. They do not lend themselves to being part of a link route and low flying area system. Nevertheless knowledge of the flow directions and choke points is valuable safety information for civil pilots and should be readily available. It is recommended that the Ministry of Defence and CAA should arrange for flow directions and choke points of the UK Low Flying System to be published on those topographical charts which are most commonly used by civil pilots. [Recommendation 94-2]

2.4.2   Vertical separation

FJ crews have a continuing requirement to train at high speed and low level. FJ aircrew may be authorised to fly in day VMC down to 250 feet MSD and at night, or in IMC, down to 500 feet MSD. Selected and appropriately qualified aircrew occasionally train down to 100 feet MSD, when specifically authorised to do so and only in certain tactical training areas and under strict control.

Civil aircraft involved in aerial work, which includes aircraft carrying out pipeline and power line surveys, aerial lifting, aerial photography, agricultural aviation (crop spraying) as well as air ambulance and police helicopters, also operate in the lower height bands. They do so in accordance with Rules of the Air, Rule 5 (1) (e) in most areas (see paragraph 1.17.7.1) but with a CAA authorised exemption they may fly as low as 300 feet agl. Aircraft involved in power line inspections fly even lower and can operate as low as the power lines themselves on certain occasions. The exemption from Rule 5 (1) (e) carries with it the condition that, when operating below 500 feet agl, aircraft must carry and operate a HISL. There is no requirement to operate the HISL when above 500 feet but to have such equipment fitted, which is designed to increase conspicuity, and not be required to use it when above 500 feet agl does not make the best use of such an aid. It is therefore recommended that the CAA should amend Rule 1 (1) of Rules of the Air Regulations 1991 so that the interpretation of 'anti-collision light' means, in relation to any aircraft, a flashing red or a flashing white light. [Recommendation 93-51 made on 28 September 1993]

Most of the FJ training (about 80%) is conducted between 250 feet and 500 feet agl and military aircraft are, by a considerable margin, the major users of this lower airspace. A modicum of vertical separation can be achieved by the recently introduced upper limit of 500 feet for normal FJ operations and the recent advice to aerial survey aircraft to minimise their operations below 600 feet agl. The MOD have proposed that the CAA should consider certain aerial work tasks taking place below 250 feet. The operating and safety aspects of such a proposal will need to be carefully considered. With the exception of aircraft involved in power line surveys, which are afforded a degree of protection by the pylons and wires themselves acting as known obstructions and whose positions are published on aeronautical charts, aircraft involved in low level survey operations and which are not subject to CANP notification (see paragraph 1.17.4) should be encouraged, where possible, to operate above 500 feet and preferably at 700 feet agl for the majority of their operations. For these reasons it has been recommended that the Civil Aviation Authority should circulate a notice to those AOC holders involved in aerial surveys recommending that where practical they operate in the height band of 500 feet to 700 feet thus providing a degree of vertical separation from high speed low flying military aircraft which will generally operate below 500 feet. [Recommendation 93-47 made on 28 September 1993]

2.5   Procedural separation

2.5.1   Civil aircraft notification procedure (CANP)

Besides physical separation it is also possible to arrange procedural separation. CANP has been available to civil operators since 1974. The opportunity to use CANP in the circumstances of this accident did not arise because pipeline and power line inspection flights had been specifically excluded from the procedure (see paragraph 1.17.3). In 1984 it was at the instigation of the principal operator at the time, and with the full agreement of the British Helicopter Advisory Board (BHAB), that such inspection flights were excluded from the system. Experience by the main operators had shown that there was considerable difficulty in providing, at the necessary notice, sufficiently accurate times and positions for aerial survey activities. This was in large measure due to the extensive areas covered which did not lend themselves to the 'point target' nature of CANP. Whether or not a notification procedure would have prevented this accident cannot be determined. Shortly after the accident NATS initiated a review of CANP from which a notification system more applicable to pipeline inspection flights was devised (PINS see paragraph 2.5.2.2 below). This suggests that there has always been a need to notify military users of the low level airspace about aerial survey flights and voluntary withdrawal from CANP may, with hindsight, be seen to have been unwise. Despite its limitations it must have had some benefit.

The relatively low number of daily CANP notifications (seldom more than five per day) tends to confirm a number of assumptions about the procedure. Firstly, it may be that typical users of this airspace such as microlight aircraft, hot air balloons, aerial application aircraft and minor air displays are adequately covered by other procedures such as the NOTAM system and by the creation of protected airspace. Secondly, the civilian pilots who would be well advised to use the procedure may be unwilling to compromise their flexibility of operation by the somewhat exacting terms of the notification for time, area and forewarning. Thirdly, the low usage rate of the procedure may imply a lack of confidence in it by those to whom it is made available based on their past experience of close encounters with FJs who may inadvertently miss the sighted civil traffic by quite narrow margins. The procedure itself only specifies a vertical avoidance by 300 feet. For this reason it has been recommended that the current review of Civil Aircraft Notification Procedures by the CAA should examine the existing separation criteria concerning over flights of sites notified under the procedure. [Recommendation 93-52 made on 28 September 1993]

2.5.2   Pipeline Inspection Notification System (PINS)

Experience of operating within the provisions of PINS, which became operational on 25 October 1993, will decide its own effectiveness. It has to be recognised that this procedure applies to a quite specific type of activity within the low level airspace and other users remain without its protection. There is a growing level of aerial activity associated with the Police and Helicopter Emergency Medical Services aircraft. By definition these flights are entirely random and unforeseen and therefore cannot fall within any system of prior notification. These airspace users must rely on some of the other collision preventative measures which are recommended in this report.

2.5.3   System effectiveness

Both notification systems (CANP and PINS) are essentially a one-way flow of information in that participating pilots are able to inform the military low flying system of their intentions but, apart from an acknowledgement, civil pilots must take on trust the guarantee that they will be avoided. There is no 'confidence check' built into the system. It is both impractical and operationally unsuitable for the military low flying programme to be published on a daily basis. There is a requirement for some feedback to civil operators that the procedural separation systems are effective. The current avoid criteria for CANP permits FJs to avoid a notified area by as little as 300 feet vertically. Whilst the FJ pilot's perception of such separation is probably adequate it almost certainly is not for the civil light aircraft pilot. In recent airmiss reports it has been impossible to decide whether the FJ pilot was deliberately avoiding by the minimum or whether the avoidance was the best that could be managed following a late sighting. A dialogue between the users of low level airspace must be established so that all users can have confidence in the procedural separation systems.

It is therefore recommended that the Ministry of Defence publish annually statistics relating to the monthly number of CANP and PINS flights which are filed together with any significant reports of failures in the system whether arising from breaches of the notified areas by military aircraft or non-compliance with the notification by civil aircraft. [Recommendation 94-3]

2.6 Improving visual acquisition and recognition times with technology

The problems of visual target acquisition, which is the fundamental requirement for 'see-and-avoid', have been re-stated and examined in this report. The margins available at the present speed of FJs at low level are such that technological aids are essential in order to further reduce the risk of collision.

The report at Appendix B examined the reflectance of the two colours of the helicopter's fuselage and the effects that a 2,000 cd HISL had on the probability of visual detection. Work was also carried out on the reflectance of the grey / green camouflage of the Tornado. Estimates were made of the likely detection time for the HISL on the JetRanger and a hypothetical 80,000 cd beacon. The cumulative probability of detection for the HISL would pass the 50% point less than 3 seconds before impact. For the brighter light the estimate was more than 16 seconds. A graphical presentation (Appendix B, Annex A, figure 4) also highlighted the increase in detection times achieved by painting a helicopter black.

Following a recommendation by JAWG the CAA specified the fitting of HISLs to all aerial work aircraft whilst exercising the privilege of their exemption from Rules of the Air 5(1)(e). It is unfortunate that the advice then was that a light of at least 2,000 cd intensity was required. This is now superseded by advice that at least 40,000 cd and ideally 80,000 cd is recommended if such lighting is to be effective in all conditions. Suitable light sources are now available and suitable applications for light aircraft can, in principle, be developed.

Research is being carried out by MOD into conspicuity enhancing aircraft lights and the adoption of high conspicuity colour schemes for certain classes of aircraft (notably training ones). This research is being conducted in association with the testing of an electronic CWS. A combination of increased conspicuity measures (paint schemes and enhanced lights), an effective CWS and a successful electronic strobe detector would do much to reduce the risks involved.

It is therefore recommended that the Ministry of Defence should give a high priority to the development and introduction of technology which provides low flying military FJs with an aircraft collision warning system, and the CAA should give similar priority to the research project for an electronic strobe detector. [Recommendation 94-4]

2.7   Air-to-air communications

It is significant that, under existing arrangements, joint users of low level airspace have no compatible method of communicating with each other. Civil aircraft communicate using the VHF frequency band while military aircraft generally use UHF frequencies. In civil VFR operations, taking place in the open FIR and without a Radar Information or Advisory Service being available [11], pilots rely to a considerable extent on intelligent monitoring of local VHF frequencies, perhaps a major aerodrome approach control or a Lower Airspace Radar Service (LARS) or a Flight Information Service (FIS). Much useful traffic information can be gleaned by listening to ATC instructions, position reports and service requests by other aircraft flying in the vicinity. This is a subtle and informal method of building up a mental picture of the traffic situation and one which applies equally in the crowded controlled airspace of a Terminal Manoeuvre Area.

Similarly, military aircraft can benefit from monitoring their own traffic pattern and flow on their UHF frequencies but they have several other important tasks, such as formation control, range work and tactical information, which also require the use of their radios. There is a practical limit to the number of frequencies that a crew can operate simultaneously and monitoring VHF frequencies may not be routinely feasible. Military ATC controllers often transmit simultaneously on VHF and UHF when communicating with either civil or military aircraft but pilots monitoring either frequency band can only hear one half of the conversation i.e. they cannot hear the other aircraft. This denies them much useful information.

By the use in the open FIR of these different and incompatible frequency bands there is, quite clearly, a communications gap. The ability of both military and civil aircraft to monitor each other's air traffic information could contribute towards deconfliction although it is acknowledged that, because of the large areas traversed by FJs in a short time, the validity of traffic information will be of short duration. Also an 'open' frequency lacks the discipline imposed by positive

---

[11]   Radar Advisory Service is seldom available below 2,000 feet because of limitations in radar coverage.

control and unnecessary 'chatter' can degrade its effectiveness. As a contribution towards greater deconfliction and despite these obvious limitations as well as those caused by the lack of radios in many gliders, microlights and hang gliders, terrain screening of the radio signal and limited range at low level, it is desirable that all aircraft operating in the open FIR should have the facility to listen in to and to make 'blind' [12] transmissions for the benefit of all other users in the vicinity. It is therefore recommended that the MOD and the CAA should examine the existing ATC communications available to civil /military aircraft operating in the open FIR to see whether the incompatibility of frequency bands adversely affects flight safety. [Recommendation 94-5]

2.8   Summary

The Tornado and JetRanger collided because of a failure in the 'see and avoid' principle whereby neither pilot saw the other aircraft in time to take avoiding action. The Tornado was fortunate in being able to land at a nearby airfield despite having sustained considerable damage. The JetRanger was most unlikely to have been able to survive the catastrophic loss of its tail rotor assembly and stabiliser.

UK aviation policy permits use of the low level airspace in the open FIR by both civil and military aircraft but there is an incompatibility, based largely upon performance and operational differences, between the joint users of the low level airspace. The degree of reliance on the 'see-and-avoid' principle in the open FIR for the deconfliction of aircraft of widely differing performance is inappropriate. Physiological limitations which contribute to the inadequacy of 'see and avoid' may be reduced by improvements in visual acquisition through the optimum use of paint schemes and the installation on aircraft of brighter lights.

Several other measures need to be implemented to reduce the risks of collision and near misses. The surest way to avoid collision is through physical separation but this ideal is unlikely to be realised because of political realities. Some deconfliction can be achieved by means of notification procedures (CANP and PINS) and with the assistance of ATC units, when available, and a common communications frequency. The recent system providing for the notification, co-ordination and vertical separation of pipeline inspection flights (PINS) was introduced on a trial basis and experience of its use will determine its effectiveness. Research into the development of a collision warning system and electronic strobe detectors is in progress but neither system is likely to be in widespread service for a number of years. Different frequency bands (UHF and

---

12   A 'blind' transmission occurs when a pilot has not established a communication link with either an ATC unit or another aircraft but where the pilot deems it prudent to make a broadcast of his position and intentions.

VHF) used for air traffic communications by military and civil aircraft do not permit the exchange of position/intention information or routine traffic monitoring by the respective airspace users.

3   Conclusions

(a)   Findings

(i)   Both aircraft were operating in accordance with their respective regulations and their crews were adequately rested, properly briefed and suitably qualified.

(ii)   Both aircraft involved were airworthy immediately prior to the collision.

(iii)   The collision occurred in good weather with excellent visibility.

(iv)   The Tornado pilot was unlikely to have sighted the JetRanger until about 5 seconds before the collision. Research shows that at least 10 seconds are required for effective avoiding action to be taken.

(v)   The pilot of the JetRanger had just completed an orbit of a ground based target and his attention was probably still directed at this. If he had seen the Tornado his ability to avoid it in the horizontal plane was extremely limited due to its relatively slow speed. However, a descending manoeuvre may have been possible, given sufficient recognition and reaction time for the helicopter pilot.

(vi)   After the collision damage to the JetRanger, which resulted in a combination of lost yaw control and an out of limit centre of gravity, was such that, despite the evident best efforts of its pilot, who was most likely disorientated, control was lost and it crashed to the ground with considerable velocity.

(vii)   Impact forces sustained by the helicopter and its crew rendered the crash non-survivable.

(viii)   Just before the impact the Tornado was on the JetRanger's right and, under the Rules of the Air, it had right of way. However, moments before, both aircraft had been head on to each requiring each to alter course. In these circumstances, involving a closing speed of 440 kt and a rapidly changing spatial relationship this aspect of the 'right of way' rules was quite inappropriate.

(ix)   There was no routine system of flight notification in force by which either aircraft could have been made aware of the likely presence of the other. CANP was not applicable to a pipeline survey flight and whether or not prior notification of the accident flight would have prevented it cannot be determined.

(x)   The decision to introduce PINS after the accident suggests that there has always been a need to notify military users of the low level airspace about aerial survey flights and the operators' voluntary withdrawal from CANP in 1984 may, with hindsight, be seen to have been unwise.

(xi)   With the exception of the Highland Restricted Area, the rest of the open FIR in the UK is not set aside for exclusive use by either military or civil aircraft. Airspace control is vested in the joint civil/military organisation of NATS.

(xii)   There are limits to the effectiveness of 'see-and-avoid' using purely visual acquisition methods. Deconfliction may be enhanced using other methods such as physical and procedural separation.

(xiii) Recognition and traffic acquisition may be augmented by technological means including electronic alerting devices and optimum paint and lighting schemes. Most of these are at an early stage of development.

(xiv)   Both aircraft were being operated in a professional manner and the collision was the tragic consequence of what must be considered a risky operational environment.

(xv)   There is limited intercommunication between military and civil aircraft because they normally operate on different frequency bands (UHF & VHF).

(b)   Causes

The investigation identified the following causal factors:

(i)   Neither pilot saw the other aircraft in time to avoid the collision.

(ii)   Incompatibility of operational modes and the unsuitability of the 'see-and-avoid' principle in these circumstances failed to ensure the necessary separation.

(iii)   There were no routine procedures, such as CANP, or facilities, such as CWS, to inform either pilot about the presence of the other aircraft prior to the impact.

40

4   Safety Recommendations

The following safety recommendations were made on 28 September 1993 and are repeated here for completeness:

93-47   The Civil Aviation Authority should circulate a notice to those AOC holders involved in aerial surveys recommending that where practical they operate in the height band of 500 feet to 700 feet thus providing a degree of vertical separation from high speed low flying military aircraft which will generally operate below 500 feet.

93-48   The Civil Aviation Authority should introduce a system of area notification of information to military crews involved in low flying training that provides the timely distribution on civil aerial activity relating to the surveying of pipelines in the UK.

93-49   The Ministry of Defence, in consultation with the Health and Safety Executive and the known energy providers, should obtain for crews involved in low level flying training suitable briefing material on the location and routes of the major pipelines within the UK. The briefing material should include any known frequency of routine inspections with provision for any variations to be notified by the operators.

93-50   Not used.

93-51   The Civil Aviation Authority should amend Rule 1 (1) of Rules of the Air Regulations 1991 so that the interpretation of 'anti-collision light' means in relation to any aircraft a flashing red or a flashing white light.

93-52   The current review of Civil Aircraft Notification Procedures by the Civil Aviation Authority should examine the existing separation criteria concerning over flights of sites notified under the procedure.

Other recommendations made as a result of this investigation are:

94-1   The Ministry of Defence should commission an operational analysis of FJ low flying training in the UK to determine whether the use of 'see-and-avoid' as the primary means of collision avoidance is satisfactory from the point of view of flight safety.

94-2   The Ministry of Defence and CAA should arrange for flow directions and choke points of the UK Low Flying System to be published on those topographical charts which are most commonly used by civil pilots.

94-3   The Ministry of Defence should publish annually statistics relating to the monthly number of CANP and PINS flights which are filed together with any significant reports of failures in the system whether arising from breaches of the notified areas by military aircraft or non-compliance with the notification by civil aircraft.

94-4   The Ministry of Defence should give a high priority to the development and introduction of technology which provides low flying military FJs with an aircraft collision warning system and the CAA should give similar priority to the research project for an electronic strobe detector.

94-5   The Ministry of Defence and the CAA should examine the existing ATC communications available to civil /military aircraft operating in the open FIR to see whether the incompatibility of frequency bands adversely affects flight safety.

R StJ Whidborne
Principal Inspector of Air Accidents
April 1994

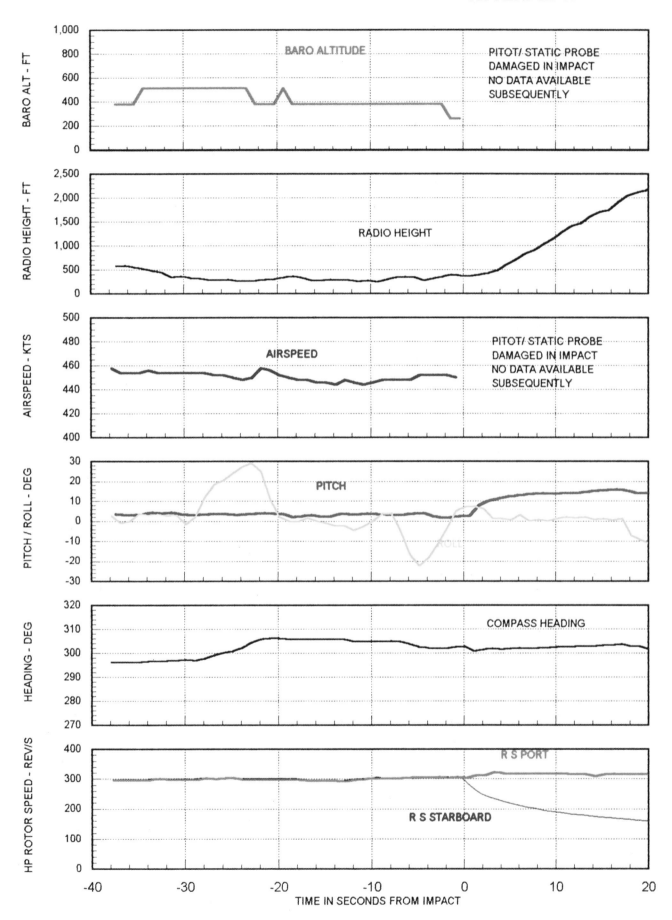

Figure 1

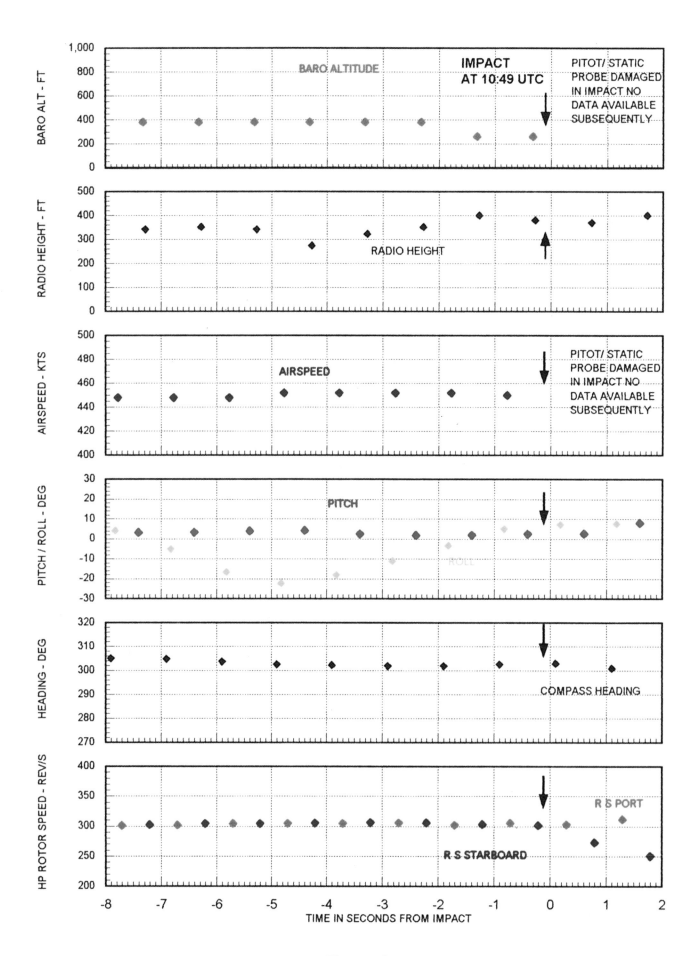

Figure 2

Derived Ground Track for Tornado starting 38 seconds before the collision

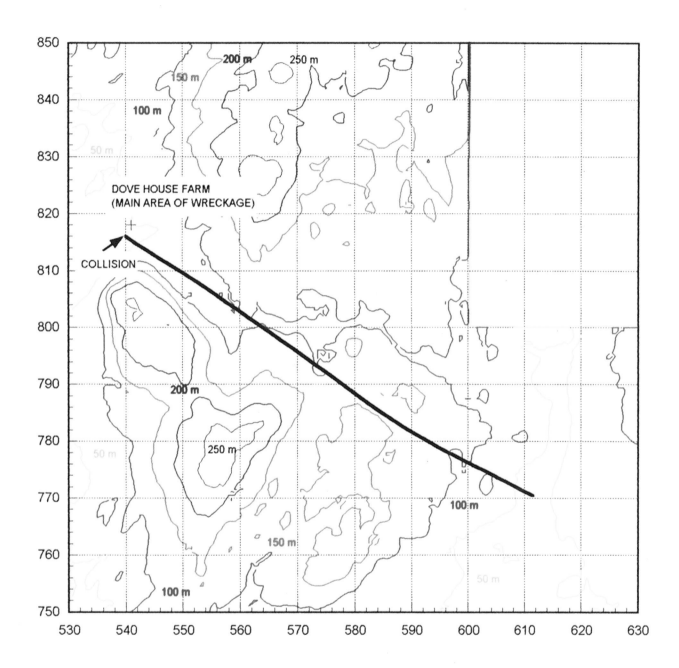

Ground Contours at 50 m intervals calculated from Ordnance Survey Digitised Terrain Data
(no data obtained for area north/east of Grid Ref 600800)

Estimated position of Collision 540816

Figure 3

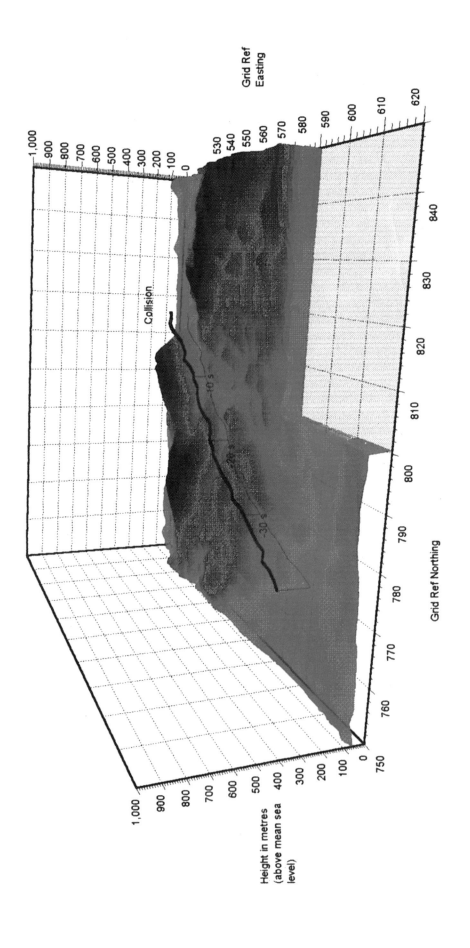

Three dimensional view of the estimated track for the Tornado

Surface plot calculated from Ordnance Survey Digitised Terrain Data (no data obtained for area north/east of Grif Ref 600800)

Figure 4

RAF IAM Accident Report 002(P)/93

Mid-air collision: Tornado and Jet Ranger on 23 June 1993

1. **Resume of events**

The crew of ZG754 were flying as number two on a pairs low level
sortie. Approaching a turning point to the south of Kendal, they entered a
valley heading 300°, and the leader passed behind a hill to their south in
battle formation. As they emerged from the valley, the aircraft struck a
Jetranger helicopter engaged in pipeline inspection. The helicopter was
destroyed and the crew of two killed. The Tornado was successfully
recovered despite serious damage.

2. **Discussion**

This report will concentrate on factors involved in visual look out, there
being no other human factors of note to consider.

Figure 1 shows the positions of the two aircraft in the last 25s before the
collision. In the case of the Tornado these are derived from ADR data; for
the helicopter they are based on eye-witness reports and so are less
reliable. Contours on a hill to the south are also marked. Figure 2
represents the view from the Tornado pilot's position and shows that the
helicopter would have been generally in the head up display (HUD) field
of view throughout the critical period (initially about 4° right of centreline,
eventually about 9° left of centreline). At about five seconds from impact
the helicopter could have been sufficiently close to the left forward
windscreen strut to impede detection. From the navigator's point of view
(Figure 3) the helicopter would have been concealed behind displays and
other equipment, and the potential for him to contribute to visual search in
the critical area was negligible.

Figure 1

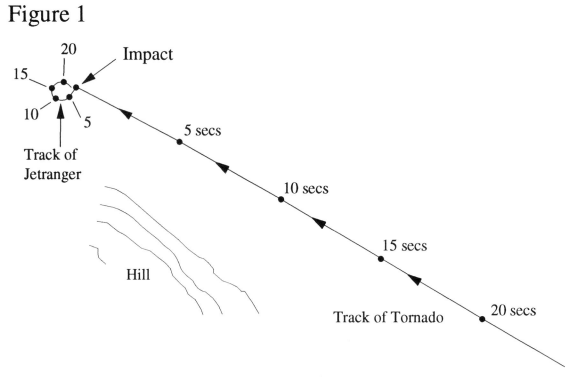

Relative positions of Tornado and Jetranger prior to impact

Annex A describes the procedure adopted to arrive at estimates of the detectability of the Jetranger during the 25s preceding the collision. Figure 4 presents a summary of these estimates. It shows curves for the cumulative probability of detection assuming both visors and clear visor only in use. A range of assumptions (specified in Annex A) are involved in these estimates. Both aircraft had high intensity strobe lights (HISLs) showing, but these would have made a negligible contribution to conspicuity becoming readily detectable probably less than three seconds from impact.The curves in Figure 4 represent a best guess at the performance of a reasonably diligent observer engaged in unrestricted visual search over a reasonable area (90° by 20°). There is evidence in a timely pull up to avoid birds during the flight down the valley that the Tornado pilot may properly be regarded as such an observer. A factor not allowed for is the effect of information displayed in the HUD. The width of lines in this display was similar to the apparent size of the helicopter during most of the critical period. Although it is not possible to estimate the magnitude of the effect, it is clear that clutter and even obscuration would have reduced the likelihood of early detection of the conflict.

It is apparent in Figure 4 that the helicopter was effectively invisible until about 17s from impact. The cumulative probability of detection then rises slowly, but stagnates at I-13s to I-8s when the aspect of the orbiting helicopter reduces its conspicuity to negligible values (i.e. the probability of detection was close to zero). During the final five to seven seconds the cumulative probability rises steeply (and the instantaneous probability is substantial). The chances of detecting the helicopter would have been good unless:

(a) the helicopter was obscured; or

(b) the pilot's gaze was positively directed away from the helicopter during this period.

There is evidence for the first of these possibilities in Figure 2, particularly if the pilot's head movements changed the apparent relationship of the left forward windscreen strut to the helicopter. As for the second, at about five seconds to go the Tornado was emerging from the valley and an uninterrupted line of sight to the formation leader became possible. The Tornado pilot looked left in order to re-acquire the leader in time for their planned turn to the north, and did not see the helicopter.

3.   **The view from the helicopter**

Given that the helicopter spent most of the 25s before impact orbiting a party of workmen, there was only a brief opportunity for the crew to scan the area from which the Tornado was emerging. This opportunity started shortly before completion of the orbit (when the helicopter was orientated towards the valley), and continued after it had rolled out on a northerly heading. Between these two periods, the pilot's view to the south west would have been restricted by the helicopter's roll angle. A scan covering a relatively large area (180° by 30°) and starting at 15s from impact results in a probability plot as shown in Figure 5. On this basis, and given that the helicopter pilot was wearing prescription sunglasses, the cumulative probability of detection before he went belly up to the Tornado could have been as low as 0.35 (depending on the darkness of the sunglasses). Without sunglasses there would have been a better chance of detecting the conflict in good time, but Figure 5 is probably an optimistic estimate of the performance to be expected of the helicopter pilot given the demands on his attention during the critical period.

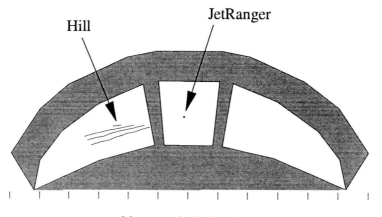

20 seconds before impact

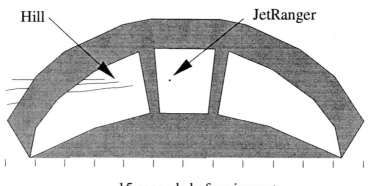

15 seconds before impact

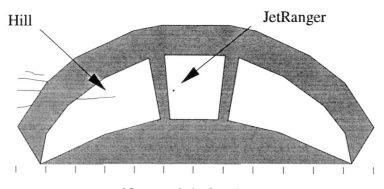

10 seconds before impact

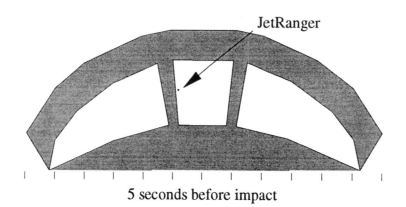

5 seconds before impact

Figure 2: Pilot's view

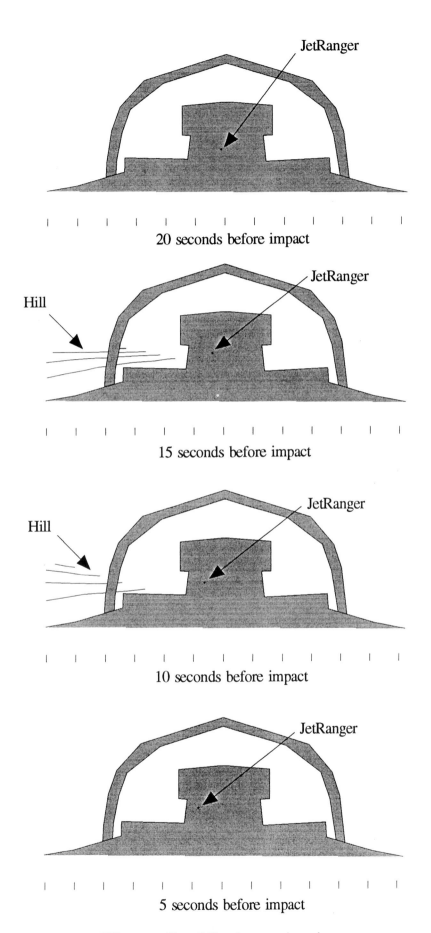

Figure 3: Navigator's view

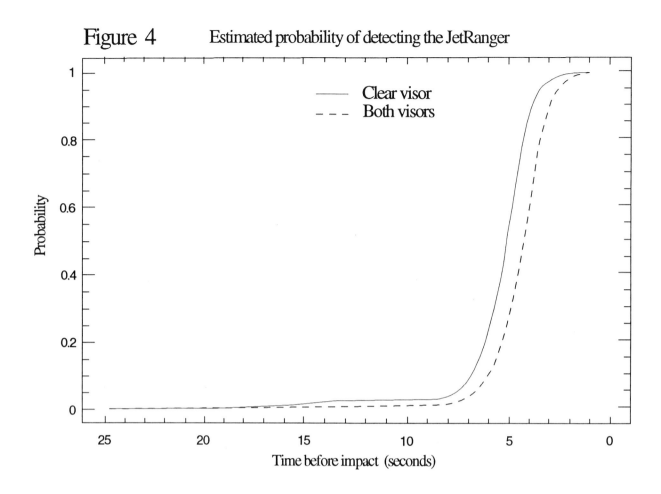

Figure 4   Estimated probability of detecting the JetRanger

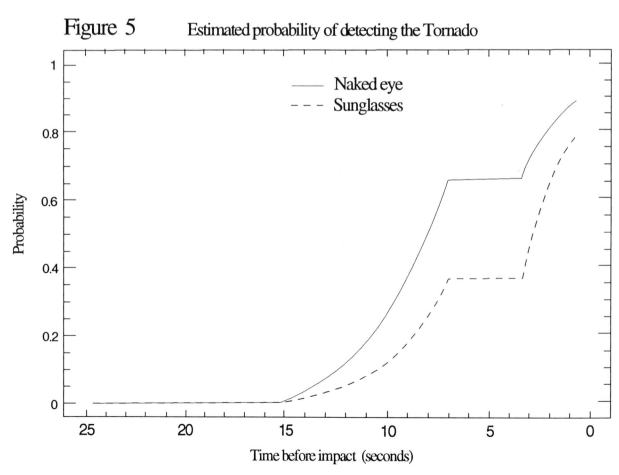

Figure 5   Estimated probability of detecting the Tornado

4. Conclusions

The circumstances of this accident illuminate the general problem of collision avoidance. Given the difficulty of detecting small aircraft, a fast jet pilot needs to sweep his forward sector roughly every five seconds - including head movements to clear canopy obstructions - in order to have a reasonable chance of avoiding conflicts. This is clearly a tall order given the other demands on his attention at low level. The pilot of a slow moving aircraft needs to scan an even wider area. It is possible to enhance the conspicuity of aircraft by a suitable choice of paint scheme and by the addition of sufficiently bright lights. (Lights considerably brighter than HISLs are currently being inves-tigated.) The risk could also be reduced by ensuring better co-ordination between operators in the lower airspace. Collision warning systems would enhance the effectiveness of visual look out, but are unlikely to prove a complete solution unless employed in combination with improvements in aircraft conspicuity.

J W Chappelow
Principal Psychologist
Psychology Division
9 July 1993   for Commandant

References

A. Chappelow, J W and Belyavin, A J. Random mid-air collisions in the low flying system. RAF Institute of Aviation Medicine Report No. 702, April 1991.

B. Chappelow, J W and Belyavin, A J. A trial to assess aids to conspicuity. RAF Institute of Aviation Medicine Report No. 723, July 1992.

C. Camouflage handbook. Avionics Laboratory, Air Force Wright Aeronautical Laboratories, Air Force Systems Command, Wright Patterson Air Force Base, Ohio. AFWALTR-86-1028, April 1986.

D. Smith, A J and Chappelow, J W. Agricultural aircraft anti-collision lighting for daytime use. Tech. Memo. FS(B)685. Royal Aircraft Establishment, Bedford, 1988.

Estimation of the probability of detection

1. **Basic data**

The Jetranger was examined in a hangar at the Air Accidents Investigation Branch, Farnborough. The reflectances of the two colours in its paint scheme were estimated by comparison with a standard reflector using a Minolta spot photometer. Intact Jetranger aircraft were examined in lighting conditions similar to those on the day of the accident, and at about the same time of day, in order to estimate the apparent reflectance of the perspex-enclosed cockpit area and side windows with the helicopter head-on to the Tornado's line of flight, and at right angles to it. The reflectances were 0.666 for white paint, 0.035 for grey, 0.275 for the front cockpit, and .028 for the side windows. The total visual area of the helicopter, and the component grey, white and perspex areas were estimated by reference to front and side plan views, and mean reflectances for front and side views were calculated.

Data were already to hand on grey/green disruptive camouflage (mean reflectance 0.127) and Tornado visual areas.

The route of the Tornado was inspected from the air (using a Gazelle helicopter) at the same time of day as the accident, and in similar weather conditions. Luminance readings were taken from a variety of positions and heights (determined by reference to the Tornado ADR) of the horizon sky and hills in the direction from which the Jetranger would have appeared, and, from the Jetranger's point of view, in the opposite direction. The hills forming the background to the Jetranger were found to have a luminance of about $3850 cdm^{-2}$ as seen from the collision point, and the sky above them was $5950 cdm^{-2}$. The sky background to the Tornado was found to be $9300 cdm^{-2}$. Illuminance measures in appropriate directions were taken at ground level. In the calculations that follow values of 44000 lux (in the direction of the Jetranger) and 14700 lux (in the direction of the Tornado) were used. The calculated apparent contrast of the Jetranger is close to zero and very sensitive to changes in assumed illuminance. The value chosen, being the maximum of those recorded, is conservative in the sense of tending to lead to higher rather than lower estimates of the probability of detection.

Estimates from other pilots in the area on the day of the accident put the visibility at more than 30km. Aftercasts from meteorological stations around the area estimated about 65km. The higher value was used in calculations. Cloud cover was about two oktas.

2.   **Probability of detection**

(a) Jetranger

At one second intervals throughout the 25s preceding the collision, the positions and orientations of the two aircraft were calculated using the Tornado's ADR data and a reconstruction of the helicopter's trajectory based on eye-witness reports. At each step the effective visual area and mean reflectance of the Jetranger as seen from the Tornado were estimated taking into account the orientation in azimuth to the line of sight:

$$A = A_f * \cos(\mathcal{T}) + A_s * \sin(\mathcal{T}) \qquad (1)$$

and

$$R = R_f * \cos(\mathcal{T}) + R_s * \sin(\mathcal{T}) \qquad (2)$$

where

	A	is effective area and R is effective reflectance.
	A_f	is frontal area and A is side area.
	R_f	is front reflectance and R_s is side reflectance.
	$\mathcal{T}$	is angle to line of sight

No account was taken of the roll or pitch angles of the helicopter. The Jetranger's apparent contrast and apparent size as viewed from the Tornado were calculated. These data were used, with interpolation, to estimate the probability of detecting the Jetranger at one third second intervals throughout the final 25s using techniques described in Reference A and slightly modified in Reference B. Assumptions were:

(i) The Tornado pilot's scan was centred on dead ahead and covered 90° by 20°.

(ii) The scan was essentially random, with shift of gaze three times a second.

(iii) The detectability of the rotors could safely be disregarded.

The accident happened in almost clear sky conditions. It was, therefore, necessary to estimate the total illumination on the Jetranger taking account of both direct and indirect sources. Reference C provided data relevant to this partition.

The cumulative probability of detection was calculated at one third second intervals for an observer with both visors in use, or only the clear visor in use. It was the Tornado pilot's practice to use only the clear visor at low level, but it is not completely certain that he did so on this occasion. Figure A1 presents these curves. The cumulative probability of detection does not exceed 0.5 until, at best, some seven seconds from impact, when the apparent size of the helicopter would have been increasing through about five minutes of arc.

In Figure A2 the curve for the clear visor case is compared with two hypothetical conditions - first, against a sky background, and second, for a helicopter always side on to the line of sight. The comparison suggests that circumstances did conspire to make the Jetranger somewhat less detectable than it might have been, but not by an enormous margin. Bear in mind also that the accident happened close to mid-summer, close to noon, with only slight cloud cover, and excellent visibility.

(b)   Tornado

Essentially similar methods were used to estimate the detectability of the Tornado from the Jet Ranger's position. In this case assumptions were:

(i) A scan area of 180° by 30°, centred on dead ahead.

(ii) The scan was essentially random, with shift of gaze three times a second.

(iii) Relevant scanning was initiated at 15s from impact, interrupted (due to aircraft attitude) at 7s to go, and resumed at 3s to go.

The resulting cumulative probability estimates are plotted in Figure A3. The pilot wore sunglasses of unknown transmissivity, so the figure includes curves for the naked eye and for a transmissivity of 0.14 as likely extremes.

3.   **Conclusions**

The Jetranger was unlikely to be detected much before five seconds from impact. Thereafter the probability of detection would have risen sharply - as long as the scanning assumptions remained valid and obscuration did not play a part.

The Tornado, having better contrast and being a larger target, would have been in principle somewhat more detectable if the Jetranger pilot had had no other demands on his attention and an uninterrupted opportunity to scan the relevant area.

4.   **Remedies**

In Figure A4 the clear visor curve is compared with predictions for helicopters with an all white paint scheme and an all black paint scheme.

Using the techniques described in References A and B estimates were made of the likely detection time for the high intensity strobe light (HISL) on the Jetranger (assumed to have an output of 2000cd) and for a hypothetical 80000cd beacon. The cumulative probability of detection for the HISL would pass 0.5 less than three seconds from impact. This is not inconsistent with the results of trials evaluating the detectability of HISLs in daylight (Reference D). For the brighter light, the estimate is more than 16s.

Figure A5 compares the clear visor case with estimated performance following a collision warning system alert at 25s to go. The pilot's scan is assumed to reduce to 30° by 10° following the alert. There is a clear benefit between I-18s and I-13s, but the changing aspect of the helicopter still renders it invisible between I-13s and I-8s. A collision warning system would, however, clearly make a useful contribution to collision avoidance on the 'see-and-avoid' principle if used in conjunction with conspicuity enhancing measures.

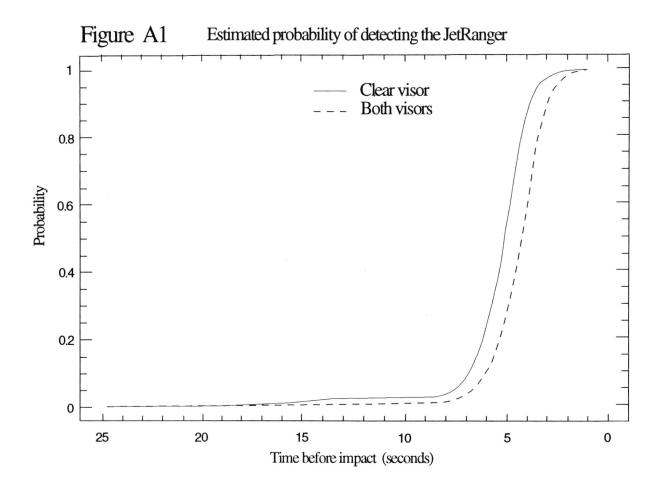

Figure A1   Estimated probability of detecting the JetRanger

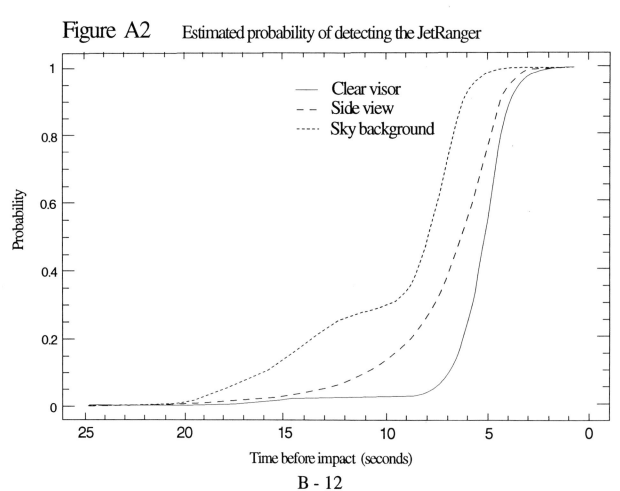

Figure A2   Estimated probability of detecting the JetRanger

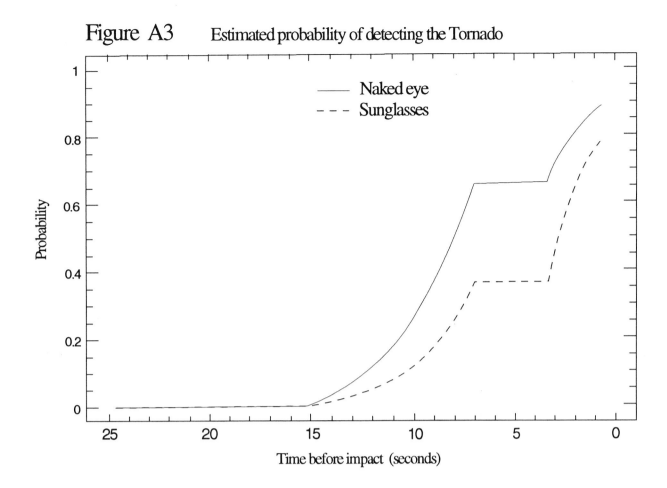

Figure A3 Estimated probability of detecting the Tornado

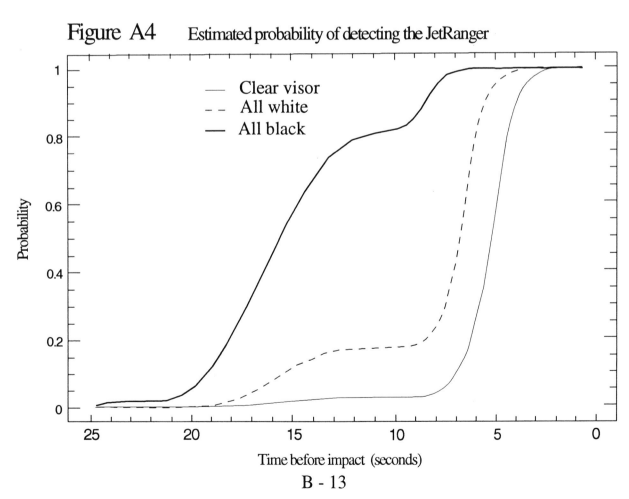

Figure A4 Estimated probability of detecting the JetRanger

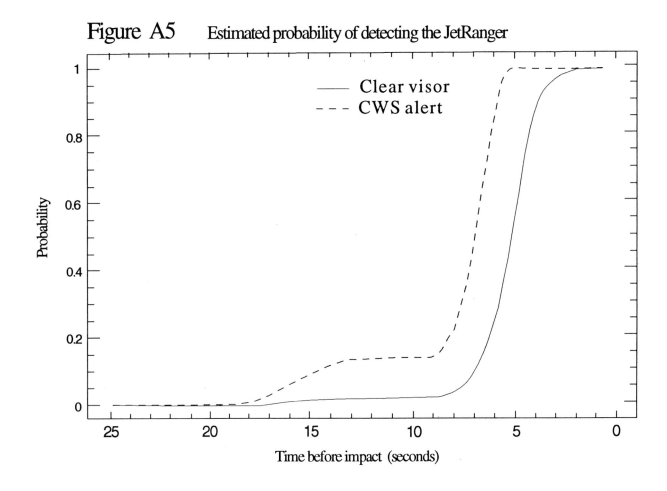

Figure A5   Estimated probability of detecting the JetRanger

B - 14

LIMITATIONS OF THE SEE-AND-AVOID PRINCIPLE

[A summary of the Bureau of Air Safety Investigation Research Report on the Limitations of the See -and -Avoid Principle]

1. Role of see-and-avoid.

See-and-avoid serves three functions:

a. Self-separation of aircraft outside controlled airspace.

b. As a separation procedure for VFR aircraft in controlled airspace. This procedure only operates when the pilot can see the traffic and is therefore significantly different to other types of see-and-avoid which may involve unalerted searches for traffic.

c. Last resort separation if other methods fail to prevent a confliction, regardless of the nature of the airspace.

It is important to distinguish between unalerted and alerted see-and-avoid. In alerted see-and-avoid, the pilot of an aircraft in controlled airspace is assisted to sight the traffic and an important back up exists because positive control will be provided if the traffic cannot be sighted. Unalerted see-and-avoid on the other hand, presents a potentially greater safety risk because it relies entirely on the ability of the pilot to sight other aircraft. For these reasons the following paragraphs concentrate on unalerted see-and-avoid. However, many of the problems of unalerted see-and-avoid apply equally to alerted see-and-avoid.

2. Potential for mid-air collisions.

The probability of a mid-air collision in a given airspace grows faster than the traffic growth. One of the factors which determines the probability of a collision is the number of possible collision combinations in a particular airspace. The number of possible collision pairs is given by the formula: $P = N \times (N-1)/2$ where N is the number of aircraft operating in a given airspace. For example, with only two aircraft there is only one possible collision pair, with five aircraft there are ten possible pairs and with ten aircraft there are forty five. The figure illustrates the increase in possible collisions which accompanies increasing traffic density .

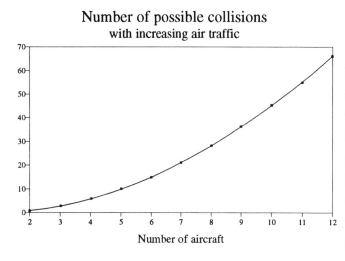

Fortunately, the frequency of collisions has not increased as steeply as figure 1 would suggest because various safety systems have prevented the full expression of the collision potential. Air traffic services (ATS), flight rules and visual sighting are three such systems.

Figure 1

3. Reliability of see-and-avoid.

See-and-avoid has been described as a maritime concept originally developed for slow moving ships which is now out of place in an era of high speed aviation.

There is a growing case against reliance on see-and-avoid. A report released in 1970 concluded that although see-and-avoid was often effective at low closing speeds, it usually failed to avert collisions at higher speeds. It was estimated that see-and-avoid prevents 97 percent of possible collisions at closing speeds of between 101 and 199 knots but only 47 percent when the closing speed is greater than 400 knots.

A 1975 Federal Aviation Administration (FAA) study concluded that although see-and-avoid was usually effective, the residual collision risk was unacceptable. Accident investigations in Australia and in the U.S. are increasingly pointing to the limitations of see-and-avoid. The Americans, having recognised the limitations of the concept, are looking to other methods such as the automated airborne collision avoidance system (TCAS) to ensure traffic separation. TCAS equipment carried on board an aircraft will automatically provide information about any nearby transponder-equipped aircraft which pose a collision threat. It is planned that by the mid 1990s all large civil passenger aircraft operating in the U.S. will be fitted with this system.

Perhaps the most damning evidence against see-and-avoid comes from recent trials carried out in the United States which have confirmed that even motivated pilots frequently fail to sight conflicting traffic.

In one of these studies, twenty four general aviation pilots flew a Beech Bonanza on a VFR cross country flight. The pilots believed that they were participating in a study of workload management techniques. In addition to providing various information to a researcher on the progress of the flight, the pilots under study were required to call out any traffic sighted.

The pilots were not aware that their aircraft would be intercepted several times during the test by a Cessna 421 flying a near-collision course. The interceptions occurred when the Bonanza was established in cruise and the pilot's workload was low, however, the Bonanza pilots sighted the traffic on only thirty six out of sixty four encounters - or 56 percent.

4. Steps involved in seeing and avoiding.

a. The pilot must look outside the aircraft.

b. The pilot must search the available visual field and detect objects of interest, most likely in peripheral vision.

c. The object must be looked at directly to be identified as an aircraft. If the aircraft is identified as a collision threat, the pilot must decide what evasive action to take.

d. The pilot must make the necessary control movements and allow the aircraft to respond.

Not only does the whole process take valuable time, but human factors at various stages in the process can reduce the chance that a threat aircraft will be seen and successfully evaded. These human factors are not 'errors' nor are they signs of 'poor airmanship'. They are limitations of the human visual and information processing system which are present to various degrees in all pilots.

5. Limitations of see-and-avoid.

a. Looking for traffic.

Obviously, see-and-avoid can only operate when the pilot is looking outside the cockpit. According to a U.S. study, private pilots on VFR flights spend about 50 percent of their time in outside traffic scan.

The time spent scanning for traffic is likely to vary with traffic density and the pilot's assessment of the collision risk. In addition, factors such as cockpit workload and the ATS environment can influence traffic scanning.

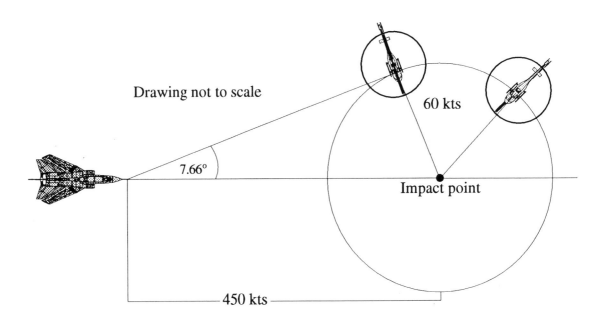

Figure 2

In the case illustrated, two aircraft are converging on an impact point at different speeds. The jet is travelling nine times faster than the helicopter and at any time proir to the collision, will be nine times further away from the collision point than the helicopter. One result of this is that the faster aircraft will always have the slower aircraft in front of it. At all times leading up to the collision, any slower aircraft with which the jet may collide will appear at a point relatively close to the centre of the jet's windscreen. From the slower aircraft's point of view, however, the jet can approach from any angle, even from part of the sky not visible in the windscreen

b. Workload.

Many tasks require the pilot to direct attention inside the aircraft. Cockpit workload is likely to be high near airports where traffic is most dense and where an outside scan is particularly crutial. Most of these cockpit tasks are essential, however some of the workload is less critical and could be performed at other times.

c. Diffusion of responsibility.

Diffusion of responsibility occurs when responsibility for action is divided between several individuals with the result that each assumes that somebody else is taking the necessary action.

d. Visual Search.

The average person has a field of vision of around 190°, although field of vision varies from person to person and is generally greater for females than males. The field of vision begins to contract after about the age of 35. In Males, this reduction accelerates markedly after 55 years of age. A number of transient physical and psychological conditions can cause the effective field of vision to contract even further. The quality of vision varies across the visual field, largely in accord with the distribution on the retina of the two types of light sensitive cells, rods and cones. Cones provide sharp vision and colour perception in daylight illumination and are concentrated at the fovea, the central part of the retina on which an object appears if it is looked at directly. Rods are situated on the remainder of the retina surrounding the fovea on an area known as the peripheral retina. Although rods provide a black and white image of the visual field, they continue to operate at low light levels when the cones have ceased to function.

Vision can be considered to consist of two distinct systems, peripheral and foveal vision. Some important differences between the two systems are that colour perception and the detection of slow movement are best at the fovea, while detection of rapid movement is best in the periphery. In daylight, acuity (sharpness of vision) is greatest at the fovea, but with low light levels such as twilight, acuity is fairly equal across the whole retina. At night, acuity is greatest in the peripheral retina.

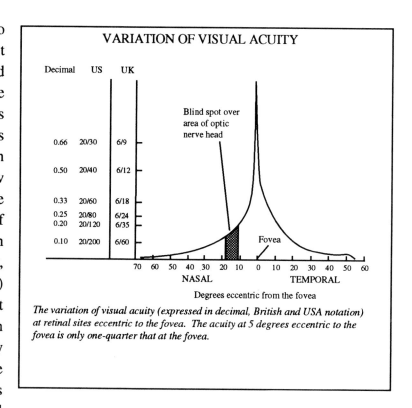

The variation of visual acuity (expressed in decimal, British and USA notation) at retinal sites eccentric to the fovea. The acuity at 5 degrees eccentric to the fovea is only one-quarter that at the fovea.

Figure 3

Figure 3 shows acuity in daylight is dramatically reduced away from the direct line of sight, therefore a pilot must look at or near a target to have a good chance of detecting it.

Peripheral and foveal vision each perform different functions in the search process. An object will generally be first detected in peripheral vision but must be fixated on the fovea before identification can occur. Searching for traffic involves moving the point of gaze about the field of view so that successive areas of the scene fall onto the high-acuity area of the retina. The eye movements in a traffic search occur in rapid jerks called saccades interposed with brief rests called fixations. We only see during the fixations, being effectively 'blind' during the saccades. It is not possible to move the eyes smoothly across a view unless a moving object is being tracked.

6. Factors limiting the effectiveness of visual searches.

a. Cockpit visibility.

Most aircraft cockpits severely limit the field of view available to the pilot. Figure 2 illustrates that a typical general aviation aircraft, because of its relatively slow speed, can be approached from any direction by faster aircraft. Visibility is most restricted on the side of the aircraft furthest away from the pilot and consequently, aircraft approaching from the right will pose a particular threat to a pilot in the left seat and vice-versa.

b. Obstructions.

Obstructions to vision can include window-posts, windscreen contamination, sunvisors, wings and front seat occupants. The instrument panel itself may obstruct vision if the pilot's head is significantly lower than the standard eye position specified by the aircraft designers. The effects of obstructions on vision are in most cases self-evident. However there are some less obvious forms of visual interference. First, an obstruction wider than the distance between the eyes will not only mask some of the view completely, but will result in certain areas of the outside world being visible to only one eye. A target which falls within such a region of monocular visibility is less likely to be detected than a similar target visible to both eyes. A second undesirable effect of a window-post or similar obstruction is that it can act as a focal trap for the eyes, drawing the point of focus inwards, resulting not only in blurred vision but distorted size and distance perception.

c. Glare.

Glare occurs when unwanted light enters the eye. Glare can come directly from the light source or can take the form of veiling glare, reflected from crazing or dirt on the windscreen.

Direct glare is a particular problem when it occurs close to the target object such as when an aircraft appears near the sun. It has been claimed that glare which is half as intense as the general illumination can produce a 42 percent reduction in visual effectiveness when it is 40 degrees from the line of sight. When the glare source is 5 degrees from the line of sight, visual effectiveness is reduced by 84 percent. In general, older pilots will be more sensitive to glare.

7. Limitations of visual scan.

The individual eye movements associated with visual search take a small but significant amount of time. At most, the eyes can make about three fixations per second however, when scanning a complex scene pilots will typically spend more time on each fixation.

An FAA Advisory Circular (90-48 C) recommends scanning the entire visual field outside the cockpit with eye movements of ten degrees or less to ensure detection of conflicting traffic. The FAA estimates that around one second is required at each fixation. So to scan an area 180 degrees horizontal and thirty degrees vertical could take fifty four fixations at one second each = 54 seconds. Not only is this an impracticable task for most pilots, but the scene would have changed before the pilot had finished the scan. Under certain conditions, the search of an area 180 degrees by thirty degrees would require 2700 individual fixations and take around fifteen minutes!

8. Limitations of vision.

a. Blind spot.

The eye has an inbuilt blind-spot at the point where the optic nerve exits the eyeball. Under normal conditions of binocular vision the blind spot is not a problem as the area of the visual field falling on the blind spot of one eye will still be visible to the other eye. However, if the view from one eye is obstructed (for example by a window post), then objects in the blind spot of the remaining eye will be invisible. Bearing in mind that an aircraft on a collision course appears stationary in the visual field, the blind spot could potentially mask a conflicting aircraft.

The blind spot covers a visual angle of 7.5 degrees vertical and 5 degrees horizontal. At a distance of around 40 centimetres the obscured region is about 1.5 cms. The obscured area expands to around 18 metres in diameter at a distance of 200 metres, enough to obscure a small aircraft. The blind spot in the eye must be considerewd as a potential, albeit unlikely accident factor. It should be a particular concern in cases where vision is severly limited by obstructions such as window posts, wings or visors.

b. Threshold for acuity.

There are times when an approaching aircraft will be too small to be seen because it is below the eye's threshold of acuity. The limits of vision as defined by eye charts are of little assistance in the real world where targets frequently appear in the corner of the eye and where acuity can be reduced by factors such as vibration, fatigue and hypoxia. Research has shown that certain types of sunglasses can also significantly reduce acuity .

There have been attempts to specify how large the retinal image of an aircraft must be before it is identifiable as an aircraft. For example an National Transportation Safety Board (NTSB) report into a mid-air collision suggested a threshold of twelve minutes of arc whereas a figure of between twenty four and thirty six minutes of arc has been suggested as arealistic threshold in sub-optimal conditions.

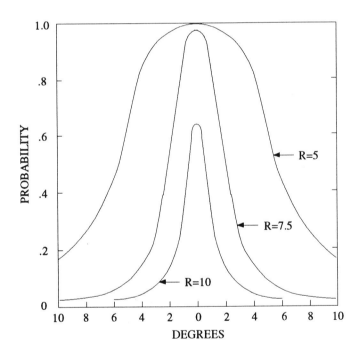

Figure 4

Unfortunately it is not possible to state how large a target must be before it becomes visible to a pilot with normal vision because visual acuity varies dramatically across the retina. An effective way to visualize the performance of the eye in a visual detection task is with a visual detection lobe such as figure 4 which shows the probability of detecting a medium sized aircraft at various ranges and at various degrees away from the line of sight. The figure illustrates that the probability of detection decreases sharply as the aircraft appears further away from the direct line of sight.

c. Accommodation.

Accommodation is the process of focussing on an object. Whereas a camera is focussed by moving the lens, the human eye is brought into focus by muscle movements which change the shape of the eye's lens. A young person will typically require about one second to accommodate to a stimulus, however the speed and degree of accommodation decreases with age. The average pilot probably takes several seconds to accommodate to a distant object. Shifting the focus of the eyes, like all muscular processes can be affected by fatigue.

d. Empty field myopia.

In the absence of visual cues, the eye will focus at a relatively short distance. In the dark the eye focuses at around 50 cm. In an empty field such as blue sky, the eye will focus at around 56 centimetres. This effect is known as empty field myopia and can reduce the chance of identifying a distant object.

e. Focal traps.

The presence of objects close to the eye's dark focus can result in a phenomenon known as the Mandelbaum effect, in which the eye is involuntarily 'trapped' at its dark focus, making it difficult to see distant objects. Window-posts and dirty windscreens are particularly likely to produce the Mandelbaum effect.

9. Psychological limitations.

a. Alerted search versus unalerted search

A traffic search in the absence of traffic information is less likely to be successful than a search where traffic information has been provided because knowing where to look greatly increases the chance of sighting the traffic. Field trials found that in the absence of a traffic alert, the probability of a pilot sighting a threat aircraft is generally low until a short time before impact. Traffic alerts were found to increase search effectiveness by a factor of eight. A traffic alert from ATS or from a radio listening watch is likely to be similarly effective. A mathematical model of visual acquisition was applied by the NTSB to a mid-air collision between a DC9 and a piper PA28. Figure 5 shows the estimated probability that the pilots in one aircraft could have seen the other aircraft before the collision.

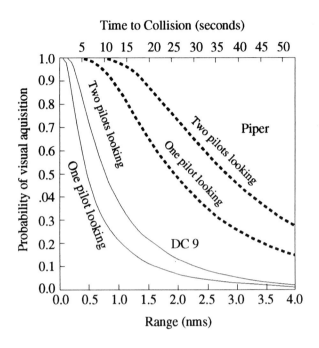

Figure 5

b. Visual field narrowing

An observer's functional field of vision can vary significantly from one circumstance to another. For example, although a comfortable and alert pilot may be able to easily detect objects in the 'corner of the eye', the imposition of a moderate workload, fatigue or stress will induce 'tunnel vision'. It is as though busy pilots are unknowingly wearing blinkers.

Visual field narrowing has also been observed under conditions of hypoxia and adverse thermal conditions. However, in aviation, cockpit workload is likely to be the most common cause of visual field narrowing.

c. Cockpit workload and visual field narrowing

The limited mental processing capacity of the human operator can present problems when there is a requirement to fully attend to two sources of information at the same time. An additional task such as radio work, performed during a traffic scan can reduce the effectiveness of the search, even to the extent of reducing the pilot's eye movements and effectively narrowing the field of view.

A number of researchers have shown that peripheral stimuli are more difficult to detect when attention is focussed on a central task or an auditory task. Experiments conducted at NASA indicated that a concurrent task could reduce pilot eye movements by up to 60 percent. The most difficult secondary tasks resulted in the greatest restriction of eye movements. Talking, mental calculation and even daydreaming can all occupy mental processing capacity and reduce the effective field of vision.

10. Target characteristics.

a. Contrast with background.

In determining visibility, the colour of an aircraft is less important than the contrast of the aircraft with its background. Contrast is the difference between the brightness of a target and the brightness of its background and is one of the major determinants of detectability. The paint scheme which will maximise the contrast of the aircraft with its background depends of course, upon the luminance of the background. A dark aircraft will be seen best against a light background, such as bright sky, while a light coloured aircraft will be most conspicuous against a dull background such as a forest.

b. Atmospheric effects.

Contrast is reduced when the small particles in haze or fog scatter light. Not only is some light scattered away from the observer but some light from the aircraft is scattered so that it appears to originate from the background, while light from the background is scattered onto the eye's image of the aircraft. The result is a 'washed out' and indistinct image.

c. Aircraft paint schemes.

From time to time, fluorescent paint has been suggested as a solution to the contrast problem. However, several trials have concluded that fluorescent painted aircraft are not easier to detect than aircraft painted in non fluorescent colours.

Trials of aircraft detection carried out in 1961 indicated that in 80 percent of first detections, the aircraft was darker than its background. Thus a major problem with bright flouescent aircraft is that against a typical, light background, the increased luminance of the aircraft would only serve to reduce contrast. In summary, particularly poor contrast between an aircraft and its background can be expected when:

(i) A dark aircraft appears against a dark background.

(ii) The background luminance is low.

(iii) Atmospheric haze is present.

(iv) Lack of relative motion on collision course

The human visual system is particularly attuned to detecting movement but is less effective at detecting stationary objects. Unfortunately, because of the geometry of collision flightpaths, an aircraft on a collision course will usually appear to be a stationary object in the pilot's visual field.

If two aircraft are converging on a point of impact on straight flightpaths at constant speeds, then the bearings of each aircraft from the other will remain constant up to the point of collision. From each pilot's point of view, the converging aircraft will grow in size while remaining fixed at a particular point in his or her windscreen.

e. Visual angle.

An approaching high speed aircraft will present a small visual angle until a short time before impact. The diagram (see Figure 6) illustrates the case of a helicopter approaching a military jet where the closing speed is 600 knots. Not all situations will be this severe, first because only about one quarter of encounters are likely to be head-on and secondly because many encounters involve slower aircraft. Given the limitations to visual acuity, the small visual angle of an approaching aircraft may make it impossible for a pilot to detect the aircraft in time to take evasive action. Furthermore, if only the fuselage is used to calculate the visual angle presented by an approaching aircraft, i.e. wings and rotor blades are considered to be invisible, then the aircraft must approach even closer before it presents a target of a detectable size.

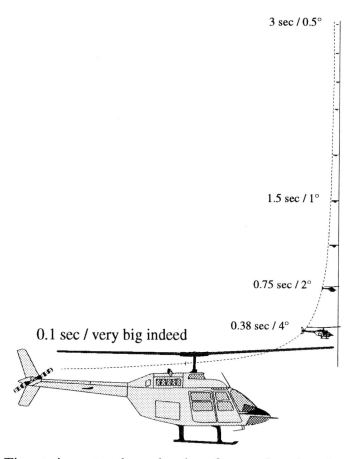

Time to impact and angular size of oncoming aircraft

Figure 6

f. Effects of complex backgrounds

Much of the information on human vision has come from laboratory studies using eye charts or figures set against clear 'uncluttered' backgrounds. Yet a pilot looking out for traffic has a much more difficult task because aircraft usually appear against complex backgrounds of clouds or terrain. The pilot is faced with the complex task of extracting the figure of an aircraft from its background. In other words, the pilot must detect the contour between the aircraft and background.

Contours are very important to the visual system. The eye is particularly attuned to detecting borders between objects and in the absence of contours, the visual system rapidly loses efficiency. A finding of great importance to the visual detection of aircraft is that target identification is hampered by the close proximity of other objects. A major cause of this interference is 'contour interaction' in which the outline of a target interacts with the contours present in the background or in neighbouring objects. Camouflage works of course, because it breaks-up contours and increases contour interaction. Contour interaction is most likely to be a problem at lower altitudes, where aircraft appear against complex backgrounds. Contour interaction occurs in both foveal and peripheral vision but is a more serious problem in peripheral vision.

11. Anti-Collision Lighting.

a. Effectiveness of lights.

There have been frequent suggestions that the fitting of white strobe lights to aircraft can help prevent collisions in daylight. At various times BASI and the NTSB have each recommended the fitting of white strobe anti-collision lights.

Unfortunately, the available evidence does not support the use of lights in daylight conditions. The visibility of a light largely depends on the luminance of the background and typical daylight illumination is generally sufficient to overwhelm even powerful strobes. Some typical figures of background luminance are as follows:

BACKGROUND	CANDELAS PER SQUARE METRE
SKY	
Clear day	3,000.00
Overcast day	300.00
Very dark day	30.0
Twilight	3.00
Clear moonlit night	0.03
GROUND	
Snow, full sunlight	16,000.00
Sunny day	300.00
Overcast day	30 to 100.00

Figure 7

In theory, to be visible at three nautical miles on a very dark day a strobe light must have an effective intensity of around 5,000 candela (see Figure 7). In full daylight, the strobe must have an effective intensity greater than 100,000 candela. Most exsisting aircraft strobes have effective intensities of between 100 and 400 candela. Trials conducted by the US Military have generally confirmed the ineffectiveness of strobes in daylight.

A major U.S. Army study was conducted in 1970 in which observers on a hilltop were required to sight approaching helicopters equipped either with strobes of 1800, 2300 or 3300 effective candela or a standard red rotating beacon. It was found that none of the lights were effective against a background of daytime sky, however strobes were helpful when the aircraft was viewed against the ground.

FAA studies have also concluded that there is no support for the use of strobes in daylight. A 1989 FAA study of the effectiveness of see-and-avoid concluded that 'Aircraft colours or lights play no significant role in first directing a pilot's attention to the other aircraft during daytime'. An earlier FAA study considered that there was 'little hope that lights can be made bright enough to be of any practical value in daylight'. A major FAA review of the aircraft exterior lighting literature concluded that 'During daytime, the brightest practical light is less conspicuous than the aircraft, unless there is low luminescence of backgroud.

b. Use of red lights.

The use of red warning lights in transport has a long history. Red lights have been used in maritime applications since the days of sail and red became the standard colour for danger on railways. An 1841 convention of British railwaymen decided that white should represent safety, red danger and green caution. It is likely that the widespread use of red as a warning colour in aviation has come about more because of common practice than any particular advantages of that colour.

c. White lights versus red.

There are reasons why red is not the best colour for warning lights. Humans are relatively insensitive to red particularly in the periphery. About 2 percent of males suffer from protan colour vision deficiency and are less sensitive to red light than people with norrnal vision. A protan is likely to perceive a red light as either dark brown, dark green or dark grey. Any colour involving a filter over the bulb reduces the intensity of the light and field trials have shown that intensity is the main variable affecting the conspicuity of warning lights. Given a fixed electrical input, the highest intensities are achieved with an unfiltered white lamp. In a comparison of commercially available warning lights, white strobes were found to be the most conspicuous. If an aircraft does carry an anti collision light, then it should be an unfiltered white light rather than a red light.

12. Evasive action

The previous paragraphs have dealt with the 'see' phase of see-and-avoid. However, it should not be assumed that successful avoiding action is guaranteed once a threat aircraft has been sighted.

a. Time Required to Recognise Threat and Take Evasive Action.

FAA advisory circular 90-48-C provides military-derived data on the time required for a pilot to recognise an approaching aircraft and execute an evasive manoeuvre. The calculations do not include search times but assume that the target has been detected. The total time to recognise an approaching aircraft, recognise a collision course, decide on action, execute the control movement and allow the aircraft to respond is estimated to be around 12.5 seconds.

b. Evasive manoeuvre may increase collision risk

An incorrect evasive manoeuvre may cause rather than prevent a collision. For example, in a head-on encounter, a bank may increase the risk of a collision. There is a limited number of ways in which the aircraft can collide if they maintain a wings-level attitude, and the area in which the two aircraft can contact or the 'collision cross-section' is relatively small. However, if the pilots bank shortly before impact, so that the aircraft approach each other with wings perpendicular, then there is a much larger collision crosssection and consequently, a higher probability of a collision. This is not to suggest that banks are always inappropriate evasive manoeuvres, but that in some cases, evasive action can be unsuccessful or even counterproductive.

UNITED KINGDOM
AERONAUTICAL INFORMATION
CIRCULAR

AIC 156/1993

(Yellow 126)

21 October

Civil Aviation Authority
Aeronautical Information Service (AIS 1c)
Control Tower Building, LONDON/Heathrow Airport
Hounslow, Middlesex TW6 1JJ
Editorial: 081-745 3456
Distribution: 0242-235151
Content: 071-832 5459   AP 6

HELICOPTER PIPELINE AND POWERLINE INSPECTION PROCEDURES

1   Introduction

1.1   Pipeline and powerline inspection helicopters which operate in the airspace below 1000 ft agl are not normally able to predict their movements with sufficient accuracy to utilise the CANP system for advising military aircraft of their activities.

1.2   In order to reduce the potential for confliction between **pipeline** inspecting helicopters and low flying military aircraft a number of measures have been introduced including a notification system specific to the pipeline activities.

1.3   The nature of **powerline** inspections and the height at which they are flown is such that helicopters engaged on these duties are less likely to be in confliction with low flying military aircraft when actually engaged in the inspection. However, when transiting between individual tasks they are recommended to conform to the height criteria specified in paragraph 3.

2   Pipeline Inspection Notification System (PINS)

2.1   The system allows for the collation of information on pipeline inspection programmes and its distribution to military operators. It is known as the Pipeline Inspection Notification System (PINS).

2.2   Details of all inspection flights should be notified in advance to the Tactical Booking Cell (TBC) of the London Air Traffic Control Centre (Military) (LATCC (Mil)) - telephone number 0895-426701 or Freephone **0800-515544**, using the regions and/or routes shown at Annexes A and B. This information will be distributed by TBC to military operators to assist in flight planning. Amendments to notified flights should be passed to TBC as soon as they are known.

2.3   Annexe A shows the division of the country into a number of regions each of which has a designatory letter. Notification of inspections which fall within a particular region should be made using the appropriate letter. In the case of major pipelines which cross the regional boundaries each pipeline route has been allocated a letter which is shown at Annexe B, hence in the case of such an inspection flight the designating letter of the pipeline should be used in the notification.

2.4   Advice on any particularly intense military low flying activity will be notified in advance to known helicopter operators by the Manager of the Military Low Flying System in order to assist with the planning of inspections.

3   Recommended Height Profiles

3.1   Helicopters engaged on pipeline inspection flights are recommended to operate in the height band 500 ft to 700 ft agl where they will be above, and skylined to, the majority of military low flying aircraft which operate below 500 ft agl. However, since both pipeline inspection and military low flying aircraft can be expected to operate outwith these specific height bands pilots are not absolved from maintaining and applying a normal lookout and avoidance criteria. In particular, it should be noted that helicopters involved in inspections will continue, when required by the inspection, to descend to 300 ft agl in accordance with their dispensation from the provisions of the Rules of the Air Regulations 1991, Rule 5 (1) (e).

4 Implementation

4.1   The PINS will be operational with effect from **25 October 1993** and the recommended heights are effective immediately.

4.2   It must be emphasised that the procedures detailed in this Circular are advisory and that the promulgation of activities will be in the form of warnings not avoidances.

4.3   This system will be reviewed after six months operation and users are invited to forward comments or recommended improvements by **1 May 1994** to HQ NATS at the following address:

National Air Traffic Services
Airspace Policy 6
Room T1022
CAA House
45-59 Kingsway
London. WC2B 6TE

Tel: 071-832 5459

This Circular is issued for information, guidance and necessary action.

Printed and distributed by Civil Aviation Authority
Printing and Publication Services, Cheltenham, Glos.

PINS REGIONS

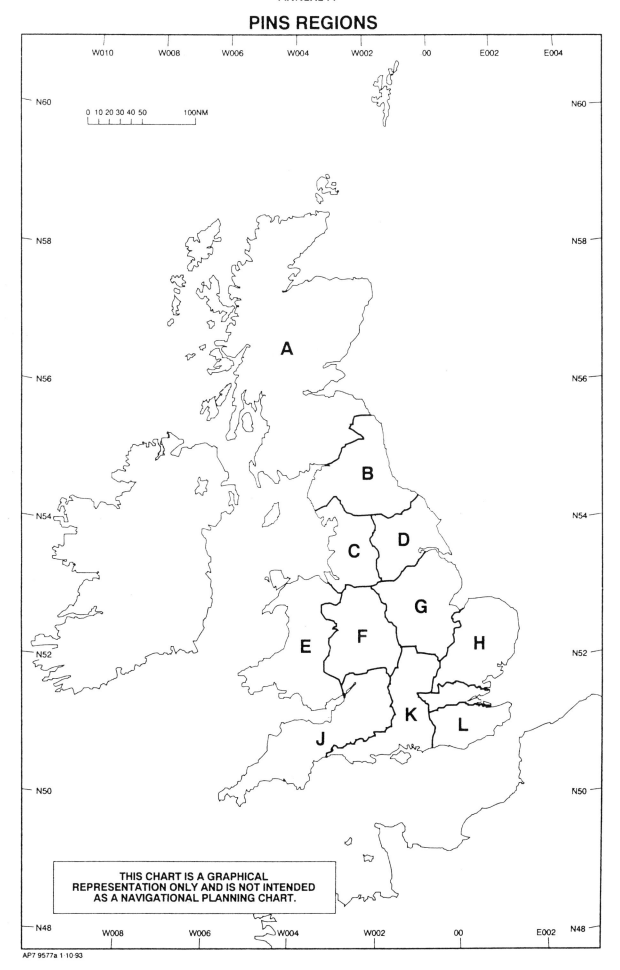

THIS CHART IS A GRAPHICAL
REPRESENTATION ONLY AND IS NOT INTENDED
AS A NAVIGATIONAL PLANNING CHART.

AP7 9577a 1·10·93

INDIVIDUAL PIPELINES

THIS CHART IS A GRAPHICAL
REPRESENTATION ONLY AND IS NOT INTENDED
AS A NAVIGATIONAL PLANNING CHART.

M - Wilton Grangemouth Ethylene Pipeline
N - North West Ethylene Pipeline
P - Trans-Pennine Ethylene Pipeline
Q - Finaline
R - Sandy/Rawcliffe
S - Stanlow/Gatwick/Thames Haven
T - Hallen/Backford
U - Hamble/Plumley
V - Milford Haven Mainline
W - Woodbridge/Hamble
X - Fawley/Avonmouth
Y - Aldermaston/Hallen

AP7 9577b 1·10·93

D - 4

MID-AIR COLLISIONS INVOLVING UK CIVIL, POWERED LIGHT AIRCRAFT, MAY 1977 TO JUNE 1993

DATE	AIRCRAFT TYPES	CIRCUMSTANCES	FATALITIES
15 May 1977	Bell 206 Tigermoth	Helicopter on takeoff collided with aircraft on final approach	1
25 Nov 1978	MS Rallye Cessna 150	Aircraft collided in visual circuit	1
8 Sep 1979	Piper PA 38 N/K	Collision whilst in cruise	0
8 Mar 1981	Robin Glider	Collided with glider during descent	0
22 Apr 1981	Quickie Cessna 152	Collided while engaged in air-to-air photography	1
30 Apr 1981	Piper PA28 Piper PA28	Aircraft collided on final approach	2
26 Aug 1981	SF25 Falke Capstan Glider	Collided 'head-on' on finals with aircraft carrying out opposing circuits	2
18 Apr 1982	Piper PA18 Glider	Tug collided with glider during descent	0
16 Jul 1983	Cessna 182 Mooney 20K	Collided during practice air race	1
29 Feb 1984	Cessna 150 Military A10	Aircraft collided 'head-on' at approximately 1,000 ft in poor visibility	1
12 May 1984	Rockwell 112 Glider	Collided at 3,000 ft in VMC	1
29 Jun 1984	Pitts Special Pitts Special	Collided during practice formation aerobatics	2
19 Aug 1984	Bolkow 209 Piper PA28	Collided during air race	2
10 Nov 1985	Cessna 152 Piper PA28	Collided at 3,000 ft	0
5 Feb 1986	Bell 47 Hughes 369	Collided in the cruise at 1,500 ft	0
29 Aug 1986	Rallye Glider	Tug collided with glider during initial climb	0
25 Feb 1987	Cessna 152 T67B	Collided at 10 ft on finals	0
10 Aug 1987	Piper PA 28 Piper PA 28	Collided with one ac climbing and one descending	0
18 Jul 1988	Piper PA38 Piper PA38	Collided during unauthorised 'dog-fighting' manoeuvres	1
6 Aug 1988	Pitts Special Yak 50	Touched wingtips during formation manoeuvre	0

DATE	AIRCRAFT TYPES	CIRCUMSTANCES	FATALITIES
4 Sep 1988	DG-400 CAP 21	Collided during takeoff / landing	0
22 Jan 1989	Cessna 182 Cessna 152	Collided over airfield	0
10 Feb 1989	Cessna 152 Microlight	Collision at 400 ft after takeoff	1
13 Nov 1990	SA 350 Ecur Bell 206	Collided during formation filming	0
3 May 1990	Grob 109 Robin	Collision with both aircraft in the cruise	2
19 May 1990	Tigermoth Piper PA28	Collision between departing and joining aircraft	4
14 Apr 1991	Great Lake N/K	Collided in cruise	0
17 Aug 1991	Piper PA 28 N/K	Collided during air race	0
29 Aug 1991	Cessna 152 Military Jaguar	Collision at low level. Cessna involved in photography. Jaguar on low level training flight	2
23 Jun 1993	Bell 206 Military Tornado	Helicopter involved in pipeline inspection. Tornado on low level training flight	2

Printed in the United Kingdom for HMSO
Dd 298128, C5, 6/94